Even Great Leaders Need Coaching: A Guidebook

by

Dr. Gary Davison

Uon,
I will finish signing this
when I see you again!

Gary

Dedication

This book is dedicated with love to the two ladies who are the bright blessings in my life... My wife, Jinger Davison, and our daughter, Gracie Davison. I love you both so much... You both inspire me to serve and be the best I can be...

"Experience is not the best teacher, feedback is..."

Gary Davison, PhD

Foreword

I am humbled to write the foreword for the book, *Even Great Leaders Need Coaching: A Guidebook,* by Dr. Gary Davison. Great schools need great leaders, and Dr. Davison's extensive experiences as a middle and high school principal places him in a unique position to present the key premises of his book. As a leader, Dr. Davison has spent a lifetime coaching and mentoring many teacher leaders and assistant principals placing them in a trajectory fully prepared to lead schools and districts. Dr. Davison is known as the "leader of leaders" in that he has had an impactful and protracted history of coaching the next generation of school and system leaders.

With broad experience as the backdrop for this book, Dr. Davison details what it takes for leaders to reach their optimum performance in schools. Dr. Davison first outlines broad areas that leaders must consider to become great at what they do. These broad areas include:

Habits of personal excellence, feedback and meta-feedback, relationships and humility, vision and direction, and planning and execution. However, Dr. Davison then leads the reader to what it means for leaders to be at the "top of their game" for each of these areas. Through Dr. Davison's conversational writing style, he puts the reader at ease, supports the self-reflection needed to be a great leader, and then challenges the reader to consider "the bottom line," presents "success indicators," and then gives examples from his experiences about what each would look like in practice. Each chapter includes a series of questions in which readers can reflect on their own performance. An added bonus in this book are the tools he has created and applied in his coaching of leaders.

Dr. Davison's book is really about coaching—coaching the very best performance out of leaders. He starts this reading journey by leading readers to think about the habits of personal excellence in what he refers to as the "excellence loop," and then leads the reader into learning how to lead with balance, accountability, confidence, resilience, honesty, civility, joy, fairness, and humility. Through his examples, success indicators, and reflective questions, the reader can walk away with better understandings about what it really takes to lead. Too many books about school leadership are presented in a deficit manner. Dr. Gary Davison approach is leadership is an asset-based proposition. How refreshing, indeed.

My biggest take-away from this book rests on his premise of leadership is a brand—without a brand, a leader cannot stand for anything. The reader can have confidence in the work presented in this text. Whether you are a principal, district leader, or aspiring leader, you will find useful information in each chapter.

It is my hope and expectation that this book will provide an effective learning experience and act as a resource for practitioners. I strongly believe that this book will lead in the development of the necessary conversations to address school leadership skills and dispositions while simultaneously supporting systems in coaching their leaders to be more successful.

Unequivocally, I recommend *Even Great Leaders Need Coaching: A Guidebook, by Dr. Gary Davison.*

Sally J. Zepeda, Ph.D.

Professor

University of Georgia

Department of Lifelong Education, Administration, and Policy

Table of Contents

Preface

Introduction

In the summer of 1966, a little boy was born. A smiling, blonde-headed kid with a penchant for shyness emerged. At the hospital that Saturday afternoon was my mother, father (more to come on that story), and grandparents. My mother, truly a candidate for sainthood later in life, was a young 15 year old when I was born. She wasn't out of the hospital very long herself as her teenage years were barely underway. I was that little boy. I'm Gary. I started life with a few strikes against me. It wasn't until later in life; where I understood I had advantages and how to employ them to my favor.

I was not a junior, even though my father and I shared a first name. My Father, Gary, and Grandfather (mother's side) did not get along. Imagine that! A 16 year-old boy who gets this man's 15 year-old daughter pregnant in the 1960's. That is the first ingredient of the recipe that would be my life. He couldn't handle his fatherly duties and decided to move back home to Nebraska. This "move" took away the largest male influence I had early in my life. So, when it came time to name me, my mother really wanted to go with her husband's name, Gary. My father's name was Gary Dave Davison. With my grandfather more than a little upset, it was a strong likelihood that it would not be Dave. So, it was the name of my grandfather, Richard. So, my name was to be Gary Richard Davison. I tell you this story as a way to set the stage of leadership models early in my life. I was not surrounded by a plethora of leaders to choose from.

I was now fatherless, living with my grandparents and teenage mother. Our family was certainly not the ideal 1960's nuclear family, but it was my normal. My mother and grandmother were primary caretakers as a young man. Unfortunately, as I turned 4, my grandfather (the only male influence) passed away from a heart attack. I idolized my grandfather, Richard Broderson. Dick, as he was called, was a man's man. Good-looking, smart, hardworking, and loving to his family. He set the baseline for what a man should be. I certainly loved and worshiped him. When he passed it really hit me hard. It was not long before my grandmother would remarry. Soon, my new grandfather would go on to be the largest positive male influence. That fact was never more evident than when I asked him, many years later, to serve as my best man.

Change would soon again happen. My mother got remarried. That marriage took us to Missouri. I eagerly had hoped for a new male presence. However, I was to be forever disappointed by the lack of relationship that existed between us. Albeit, I was in a different state, away from the grandparents that raised me, I was still searching for that male role model that I needed. Through the next few years, I went from Bernard Elementary School to Margaret Buerkle Junior High School. Finally, graduating from Mehlville High School. As an aside, I was the first of my tiny but loving family to graduate from high school. It was in these schools and during these years that I had many of my difficulties that, unknowingly, led to my life's focus as a leader. As a student, there were many teachers, coaches, and administrators that had an impact on my life. However, one of the most influential was my baseball coach. Dick Basler was a kind, funny, caring man that taught me many things that I employ to this day. I remember one time as a 12 years-old right fielder coming to the plate in a pressure situation. Runners were on first and second, bottom of the last inning and two outs. I was not the pressure-cooker kind of kid. I was petrified. As I came to the plate, Mr. Basler called a timeout and wanted to speak with me. I knew there'd be some sort of wisdom that he would tell me to make it work. However, that was not what I found. As I approached him, he knew I was freaking out. He looked me dead in the eyes and asked one question. "Hey, do you know any good jokes?" I was stunned… Did he really just ask me that? In the blink of an eye, I giggled, he rubbed my shoulder and sent me back to the plate with these parting words, "You can do this, I know you can." As if from a movie, on the third pitch, I placed a long line drive to the outfield and scored the two runners in front of me. As I came around third, I heard him say, "You got this…slide!" "Safe" the umpire yelled… That quickly we were league champions and I got the game-winning hit. I still believe to this day, it was the humor and calmness that he brought to the situation that allowed me to calm down, breathe, and encouraged me to put forth a stellar effort. There are days in the middle of crises that I employ the strategy he taught me in a pressure cooker situation. Breath and laugh.

Obviously, my last leadership lesson was not as a 12 year old. I have taken personal and professional anecdotes from my life and career and used them as examples all throughout this book. There have been many lessons learned and times where I got it wrong. However, they all lead me to this point in time. I am writing to you to share my knowledge and experiences to help you gain insight into your own leadership capacity and how to use the skills taught. If I can do it, I certainly feel confident that you can too.

As a leader, there are realms of your work that attention must be paid to reach optimum performance. Those broad areas are defined here. They are: **habits of personal excellence, feedback and meta-feedback, relationships and humility, vision and direction**, as well as **planning and execution**. Together, these areas encapsulate the totality of what I have found in my many years of leadership service to others. They hold the keys to learning great leadership skills. Each section consists of skills that can be used to hone and refine one's abilities. Again, the measure of each is dependent on the personality, experiences, work ethic, and vision of each leader. These skills comprise a tool bag to use when necessary and applicable. Some are more timely than others, while some are more perpetual than others. Again, my personality, experiences, work ethic, and vision mixed with the application of these upcoming skills have made me the leader that I have been for the last 33 years.

This book is divided up into 5 sections. Each section holds the individual skills a leader will need. Each individual skill is broken up into sections to enable the leader to navigate their own learning. First, there is an introductory summation called "**Bottom Line**". This brief section is intended to give an introduction and ease you into the concept being discussed. Next, leaders will find "**Success Indicators**". These are specific actions that leaders can employ to execute the skill. Finally, an **"Example"** of each skill is included from my life or career. The example is intended to bring a real-world application to each skill being taught. This area will get you started toward success. Each skill is intended to be a stand-alone section. Several themes are repeated within the individual skills as they are critical to great leadership. For example, feedback, communication, relationship-building, and humility are repeated actions. However, they are applied with various nuances and to varying degrees in each skill.

Introduction

Are you a school leader? Are you an emerging or aspiring school leader? Do you find yourself lacking effectiveness or feeling overly stressed? Are you stuck in a management cycle and want to learn to lead? This book will show you the skills and steps to develop a strategy to lead effectively. Additionally, this book will assist you in living a more fulfilled professional life as a leader. Ultimately, even great principals need coaching to be highly effective and live fulfilled lives.

In the first section of the book, you will learn to develop and hone your own **personal excellence**. Only through developing personal excellence will you be able to execute at the highest level possible. These characteristics will develop your potential into a formidable set of skills that you can use to lead in any organization. For example, skills like humility, resilience, confidence, fairness, civility and other skills will deepen your abilities to execute and build a leadership culture. In part two of this book, you will learn **feedback and meta-feedback** skills to grow yourself and others. Your organization's culture will be the beneficiary of these skills. For example, you will learn to lead with intention, questioning, feedback, listening, and learning among other skills. In part three of this book, you will learn to **build relationships** to lead your organization to its highest potential. For example, emotional intelligence, developing synergy, investing in others, and how to lead various generations are skills that you will develop in section three. In part four of this book you will learn to develop and use **vision and direction**. Great leaders all have a deep sense of vision and moving in the direction toward achieving the vision of the organization. For example, leaders will learn to move toward the vision, lead by example, use decision-making strategies, lead by core values, as well as many more effective skills. Finally, in part five of this book you will learn to **plan and execute**. Leaders simply cannot move an organization toward effectiveness if they are not planning and considering factors that enable execution to occur. For example, leaders will develop skills around communication, setting the conditions for success, being visible, as well as being a badass, to name just a few of the skills in this section.

These skills, among the many, helped me to develop 24 leaders into school principals and district leaders. These skills also helped me to develop my own skill set. As a result, I led the most prolific high school in the last 20 years of the state of Georgia. Additionally, our school excelled in athletics, academics, and the arts at a national level. There is a tremendous track record of achievements, however the focus on process in this book will mirror the emphasis placed on process and developing tremendous skills in staff and students. Each skill has an accompanying podcast number. The Lodge of Leaders podcast series is called the Principal Mentor Series which corresponds with each skill. Throughout this book, the terms leader and principal are used interchangeably. Consider them to be completely analogous to one another.

Testimonials

"I have known Gary Davison for several years. I watched him invest in his faculty and staff. I watched him equip the parents of his students. He is a leader worth following and a mentor worth listening to. I have used Gary's stories in two of the books I have written as illustrations of innovation and practicality. I recommend him to educational leaders anywhere."

-Dr. Tim Elmore, Founder & CEO, Growing Leaders

"Finding your niche is a goal each of us has as we live and work daily. Dr. Gary Davison most certainly has found

his...growing and mentoring leaders who already excel, into first-rate influencers. The Davison Leadership Model is second to none as evidenced by the more than 20 assistant principals, teachers, and county officials he has molded into highly successful and respected principals. I lead with confidence, creativity, and knowledge as a direct result of this innovative thinker." —--**Mr. Tom Bass, Principal, Dunwoody High School**

"Dr. Gary Davison is a gifted and talented educator who tirelessly works to help teachers and other school leaders develop their leadership skills. One example I observed firsthand is utilizing the coaching process. Whether a first-year educator or veteran, he knows the coaching process benefits all. Dr. Davison has also encouraged and supported my efforts to develop the leadership skills of teachers aspiring to become school leaders by providing the resources and time collaborating with me to develop a curriculum for the program. Dr. Davison's extensive experience and results should be obvious to anyone who knows anything about the academic and athletic prowess of Lambert High School."

-Dr. Russ Chesser, retired Principal, Pelham City High School

"Dr. Davison has the unique ability to take you on a journey where you refine your strengths and embed reflection so deeply in your work that it becomes not only how you lead, but how you improve as a leader. His coaching is custom tailored to each individual - both for where they are in their leadership development AND for how ready they are to improve their practice. Working with Dr. Davison has not only shown me the type of leader I want to be, but with his help, I continue to refine the skills needed to become that leader for my school."

-Dr. Ashley Johnessee, Principal, Haw Creek Elementary School

"Gary Davison is hands down the best principal I have ever had the opportunity to work with. I was able to serve with him on leadership teams both at the elementary and high school levels. HE is able to create a common set of beliefs that connects everyone in other school communities. One of my favorite things about working with Dr. Davison is that he always uses positive feedback to guide us toward where we need to be. He works with us to design clearly defined individual professional goals and helps us determine how to reach those goals. He has a unique talent of making every single member of a school community feel valued and respected."

-Mrs. Jennie Sheley King, Administrator, South Carolina, 3x Teacher of the Year

"Dr. Gary Davison has served the Forsyth County School System as a successful principal at multiple schools. While he has left his mark on each of them, his true legacy is the group of leaders that he developed during his time here. At one point, I can recall sitting in a meeting where four of the five high school principals in the room (including him) all had learned by working for Gary. As our system has grown, so has his "tree of leaders." We have elementary, middle, and high school principals that have worked and learned directly under him and are now leading their own schools very effectively."

"As one of his former assistant principals, I carry with me the lessons learned from him. He nudged each of us working for him to reflect on our core values. He helped us to develop a vision for our own success. Ultimately, he trusted us to own elements of school improvement where our visions could be cast, and our core values tested. The results for each one of us that matriculated to the next level of leadership were that we had real experiences that let us know who we truly were, what we valued most, and on how to bring others to fulfill a vision for success."

-Mr. Mitch Young, Deputy Superintendent, Forsyth County Schools

"I have had the privilege of Dr. Davison's mentorship and coaching for over 15 years. His focus on the benefits of a relationship-centered approach to the work, recognizing and nurturing the talents of each person in the organization, yields results that can be felt in the climate of the organization and seen in the achievements of students and employees."

-Mrs. Pam Bibik, Principal, Riverwatch Middle School,

If you apply the skills outlined in the *Even Great Principals Need Coaching: A Guidebook*, you will be prepared to lead more effectively and live a fulfilled professional life. Your influence will grow thus making you a more effective leader each day.

Let's embark on the journey to help grow your skills and lead more effectively.

PART 1:
Habits of Personal Excellence

Personal Excellence is not a destination. Rather it is a journey to be the very best version of yourself that you can achieve. It requires total commitment. A commitment to owning the deficits you know, reflecting on your performances, amending your actions based upon feedback, displaying extreme effort, and striving to attain an aspirational goal. The journey towards personal excellence is not meant to be arduous. However, growth requires change. You need to change and your skills and habits need to develop. This journey will allow for incredible growth not merely a slight improvement. The journey toward *Personal Excellence* is a true measure of a person's willingness to embrace their deficits and abilities that, ultimately, lead to their success.

Characteristics define our makeup as a person. Whether you are quiet, loud, meek, assertive, or quick-witted, each of us has a sliding scale of characteristics that define who we are. I have known effective leaders who are the quiet, deep-thinking, deliberate people who mull over and process information. Conversely, I also have known leaders that are more gregarious and open with their processes. There is not a template to which your attributes must all fit. Rather, leadership is the assemblage of who you are (attributes), the totality of your skills (talents), and the inclination to improve your performance based upon feedback (effort) that formulate your likelihood for success.

Here are a few questions to get you started on your journey as you seek to demonstrate personal excellence:

- What level of effort are you willing to give?

- How do you gather feedback from others or even yourself?

- Do you attempt to be efficient or effective?

- When you find yourself at odds between core beliefs and personal actions, where do you fall?

- What is something you are hungry to learn?

- What are you willing to sacrifice to attain your goal?

- Do you compete against yourself or against others?

- When was the last time you surprised yourself with your outcomes?

- How can I replicate my own change in perspective?

- What can I do to help others achieve more than they realize?

This evolution toward *Personal Excellence* can be summed up in a process that I developed and have used for most of my career. I call it the **Excellence Loop**. When choosing to pursue excellence in every endeavor, sacrifices must be made. The Excellence Loop is based on sacrifice, reflection, and commitment. The four pillars of the **Excellence Loop** are*: Preparation, Practice, Performance, and Process.* Let's take each of these and go a little deeper into each one.

- **Preparation**- As leaders seek to gain knowledge and understanding of their various strategies, preparation is the key to acquisition. To prepare, leaders should read books, magazines, and articles, as well as listen to podcasts, and discuss with esteemed leaders regarding strategies and skills. These texts and interactions should not be solely focused on the leader's industry. This way they will get a full range exposure to leadership from all facets and applications. Leadership is not merely a domain of business, the military, or education. Great leadership strategies can be learned from all fields. Thus, we as leaders need to be open to pursuing those opportunities wherever they may be.

In the words of Brian Tracy (2012), *"Effective performance is preceded by painstaking preparation."* Preparation is the plan to improve on new or previous performances. We seek to gain improvement on our skills and abilities. To attain excellence, leaders should place considerable effort and time in this phase. To prepare effectively is to establish the foundation of excellent performance.

- **Practice**- Once leaders have planned sufficiently, it is now time to practice the skill. To many, this may sound redundant. However, there is a clear distinction in the Excellence Loop between preparation and practice. To prepare is to establish a foundation of learning necessary to perform at a high level. To practice, however, is to repetitively perform until simulating perfection. This can be done with multiple repetitions, in various settings, at different paces, and in a formative fashion. Formative means that learning from mistakes is the short-term goal, while executing flawlessly is the greater mission. To reach this flawless execution, even the most seasoned leader must keep their skills sharp by repetitive simulation of perfect practice. To practice a skill in a sloppy or unfocused manner will not bring you closer to excellent performance. Legendary NFL Coach, Vince Lombardi once said, *"Practice doesn't make perfect, perfect practice makes perfect."* The goal is to repeat a skill flawlessly until it becomes second nature.

• **Performance**- Once a skill has reached repetitive perfection, we are ready to perform in the moment. We need to have our skills and abilities ready to go at a moment's notice. The moment is considered a summative opportunity to execute our skill. I like to think of it as "Game Day" after I have practiced a skill many times. Being ready for a performance doesn't mean we always succeed. However, we are prepared to succeed. In the words of Orrin Woodward, *"Principles are proven through performance."*

• **Process**- Once a skill has been performed, we are ready to assess the results of our performances. This is a time of positive feedback, encouragement, constructive feedback as well as self reflection. This is where true growth and learning take place. The amount of effort spent on this step is relative to the amount of growth one will likely show. If we fail to process the results, we can expect to fail replication of the skill. The performance is where the skill is executed, but the likelihood that skills will be replicated excellently is based on reflection and feedback. Nick Saban, legendary college football coach said it best, *"Focus on the process of what it takes to be successful."*

Learning a new skill and applying the strategies to perform excellently is not difficult, rather it is methodical. As an example of the Excellence Loop, let's look at learning to drive. When teaching my daughter, Grace, to drive I helped her go through the four steps of the Excellence Loop. We started with *preparation*. To prepare, Grace read the manuals and learned the functions of an automobile. She rode with us and watched lane changes, turning, signaling, and the many skills necessary to safely drive a vehicle effectively. Next, it was time for Grace to *practice* driving. Of course, she was not on a road by herself. She was in an open parking lot slowly navigating the vast spaces in a controlled manner. As she built up confidence and precision, she was able to tackle small intrusions into lanes, small roads, and our neighborhood. Once her proficiency and confidence built, she drove me onto small roads and on short trips. She was not yet ready to be alone on the trips. It was not until her practice became nearly second nature that she was unleashed to attempt a "performance".

Grace's performance opportunity came when she tested for her license. She got behind the wheel of the car. Her tester gave her commands and ran her through all of the components of the assessment. She was asked to encounter many traffic situations, parking lots, and instances only referred to in the manual. Her preparation paid off when she scored a nearly flawless score. However, that was not the end of the event. She still needed to enter the fourth step of the Excellence Loop. Upon returning to the testing center, I asked how she did and the evaluator gave me her score. I was very proud. She, however, needed to work on several items to reach the excellence level. There was feedback to process, results and scores to assess, and reflections she had to give herself. Nearly a year after the testing, she still has improvements to make, but attaining a standard higher than merely passing is uniquely important.

Lead with Passion

"Life doesn't get easier or more forgiving, we get stronger and more resilient." Steve Maraboli

BOTTOM LINE

We all remember the award-winning movie, "Rocky". In the latest installment of the series, Rocky famously said, *"It's not how hard you get hit, it's how many times you get back up."* He was referring to boxing and life. We as leaders have a different application of that famous line. We will take lumps, we will have bad days, and experience many disruptions. There are countless upset parents, irrational situations to manage unreasonable budget requests, never-ending time constraints, and the tumult of increasing expectations. No matter the challenge, we are tasked with being leaders without excuses. No leader worth their salt will use excuses to "get out of" the challenges. It is not in our DNA to do such things. However, if you find these challenges too daunting to overcome, I have some ideas here for you to help.

Do not get framed by negativity. Win despite it. Be defined by a good, positive, passionate mentality toward your work, your team, and the outcomes you desire. Your mindset is the key to being prepared for these challenges. Be passionate! If you are a glass half-full type of person and passionate for all things in your organization, then you are well equipped to handle the new challenges. I have given you five success indicators that can help you be prepared.

SUCCESS INDICATORS

Share the Jocko Willink philosophy of "Good…"

I am a big fan of Jocko Willink (2015). Jocko was a Navy Seal and is now a business consultant. He has lived through more harrowing situations than any of us can imagine. He has seen war, death, and despair. Yet he has been able to frame his thinking in a passionate, positive direction. His book, "Extreme Ownership" is the epitome of being passionate while in the midst of challenge. He often refers to a word he often gave team members when they brought him insurmountable challenges.

"He would call me up…and he'd say this and that…and I'd look at him and say…GOOD. We finally have a chance to get better…" Jocko used this one-word answer to clarify, not only the expectation of the team, but also the direction the team was going to embark. His "Good" was a loud thud to the negativity that can be brought to us as leaders. I don't think that people always intend to

be negative. It's just so darn easy for them sometimes. When difficult things arise, our tendency is to look at the tragedies that can result. We are risk averse and wish to keep ourselves away from it. I get it! But we need to use Jocko's example to discipline ourselves to not go there. We can prepare ourselves to look at the glass as half-full. We can teach our teams the same discipline. Don't entertain the negativity. Don't give it a voice. In a clear, simple, and kind manner respond to your teams with a strong positive voice. "Good...this challenge will make us better as a team."

Speak with your team about potential challenges. "What will we do when it happens?"

I firmly believe that preparation is the key to success in all things. The Excellence Loop shows us that there is a lot to gain from having conversations with members of your team about challenges that may arise. Being prepared will allow you to embrace difficulties with a smile, energy, and the passion that will inspire others. In addition to a feeling of preparedness, your passion in difficult times brings confidence in your leadership.

Actions meet words. Make them congruent and authentic.

Passionate words are necessary in challenging times, but your actions will speak volumes compared to your words. Additionally, your words have an increased meaning when accompanied by actions that reflect your words. Passionate actions are those that ease people, inspire others, and bring calmness with a sense of confidence. Smiles, handshakes, and moving deliberately and with a steady stride are all actions that reflect passion and confidence.

Stay positive. Own the difficulties. Avoid gossip.

As a leader you are the most visible and important person that people look to in a challenging time. Your every action and word will be dissected. Be obvious and clear. Don't avoid difficult questions or comments. Own the challenges. Never run from them. Gossip will breed in the absence of clear information. Be clear up front to avoid unclear expectations and information. When gossip does emerge, don't play in that sandbox. Leaders are not expected to be a middle ground. Have a strategy to deal with gossip when it emerges. Redirection is the best tool I have found. A friend once shared this strategy with me when he was confronted with a person wanting to share inaccurate information about a colleague. He simply changed the subject to something completely different than what was being discussed. It threw the offender off and clearly stated that he would not participate in such foolishness. Additionally, the offender never shared any gossip about anyone with him in the future.

Win over your troubles.

Each day, challenges will come and go, but strong leaders are ever-present. When the most difficult times present themselves, your team needs you to be the leader. They are relying on you to be stable, positive, and confident. This is the time to show tenacity in your resolve. You need to stick with strategies and priorities that will bring about a resolution. A positive resolution is one that you and your team can agree on. Seek wins, but there may be times where you need to seek neutrality. Occasionally, that can also be considered a win.

EXAMPLE

As a leader, my personal life can sometimes get in the way. In 2007, our son Will, passed away just before the start of the school year. His passing was a gut punch. As you can imagine, it is the most horrific pain any parent can suffer. It is not a momentary issue, it is a life-long pain that never goes away. However, I still had a job to do. That may sound cold and unfeeling. Please know that it is not meant to be unkind. Albeit, we still had 3000+ kids at school to plan for when they arrived on campus in a matter of days. I could not let the tragedy affect my life as a leader. I needed to find a way to compartmentalize this horrible tragedy during the day. Every moment I closed my eyes or stopped moving it was a stabbing pain to my heart. To this day, I still deal with the pain of his loss. However, it became rocket fuel for me. I became obsessed with treating each student as my own child. The child I had very recently lost. It was my coping strategy to be capable of getting through each day. I have since been told it was not a healthy way to proceed, but it worked for me. I would do for them what I wanted for him. I took the words of Rocky Balboa to heart. I was emotionally, and sometimes physically, knocked down. It took every ounce of strength I had. But, I felt my son would have wanted me to do that for our family, our school, and our community.

Lead with Balance

"You are no good to anyone if you can't take care of yourself." Gary Davison

BOTTOM LINE

Principals can't effectively lead others if they are unbalanced. Leaders, keep yourselves healthy. Truly healthy means keeping one's self sharp and prepared for anything needed spiritually, physically, and mentally. How many times have you been on an airplane and heard the pilot remark that you must place the oxygen mask on yourself prior to helping others around you? The first time I heard this I thought it was very strange. However, after being a leader for 25 years, I now agree with this statement. As a leader, I cannot help others around me if I am not in top condition myself. That being said, I need to have a plan to stay strong in all aspects to be able to support and serve my organization.

I have listed five success indicators that will start you on the path to being a stronger leader for your team.

SUCCESS INDICATORS

Know what your mind, body, and spirit need. When you were at your best what did you need?

Only you can know what you need. However, there are some basic truths when it comes to overall health. One truth is that type-A persons, most likely to be school principals, are avoiders of self care. We are notoriously burning the candles at both ends in the effort to serve others. That is very noble, but not very smart. The three categories of health are: Mind, Body, and Spirit. In today's world, we often hear this being called "Self Care". It sounds very complicated and quite involved. I understand the need for such a term, but I think more simply about the concept. I tend to boil it down conceptually. Worry less, move more, and pray often. Let's take a look into the three categories more closely.

Mind- The mind is our most used and most powerful tool. Stress, worry, panic, boredom, and distraction can be but a few of the deterrents to our mind's effectiveness. None of us can wave a magic wand and hope these go away. There are effective strategies to cope with an unusual amount present in our minds. Therapy, relaxation, as well as positive and healthy antidotes are available for each.

Of course, I have only come to realize this after many years of coping with stress to a major degree. Each day, I would come home after an incredibly stressful day only to be unproductive and unhealthy. Eating too much, watching television and being sedentary contributed to my unhealthy lifestyle. All of these, while feeling good at the moment, were destructive to my ability to cope with the impending doom of an unhealthy mind. Eventually my high levels of stress took its toll. I found myself being referred to a

19

cardiologist for stress-related concerns, gaining too much weight to be considered healthy, and not treating my family with the respect they deserved. However, I felt justified as it was in the service of others. Albeit, I was not serving them as well as I could. I was fooling myself. I'm only glad that I realized this in time to be able to correct some of these behaviors. It took the shutdown of our school in 2020 for me to realize this. I was bound to not let this virus affect my overall life. In turn, I became vigilant to address the three areas. In particular, I tackled my stress levels by intentionally slowing down my thinking and breathing. I found quite a reduction in my overall stress. Add to that, my relationships at home improved as I was much more pleasant to be around.

Body- When our bodies are not balanced with our other areas, we are creating an issue like a loose thread on a sweater. It is fine for a while, but eventually the thread gets pulled and begins to slowly destroy the garment. Eventually, the cloth is tattered and too worn to be any good to wear. Our bodies are the same. Neglecting my physical health was fine while I was very young. As the years piled up, my back problems (from previous injuries and too much weight), my knee problems (from previous injuries and inactivity), and my weight became issues I could no longer avoid. The aforementioned cardiologist scare added to this concern. Again, the Pandemic provided me with the necessary wake up call to address these issues head on. I began drinking more water, finding workouts that I enjoyed each day, and eating a healthy diet. In a few months, my weight was in control, my vigor was high, my attitude was much better and I handled stress well. These three areas all work hand in hand to help or hurt one another. I was able to compound my efforts by addressing these together. I was becoming a much better leader by being healthier.

Spirit- The need for a leader to be healthy spiritually does not mean you have to become a religious person. It means that you are seeking fellowship and guidance with a higher power. Your selection of higher power is a personal decision. However, my choice to become a more faithful Christian was a very decisive choice for me. I have been spiritual for a number of years, however the death of my son and the focus on my health in the Pandemic refocused my efforts to being guided by my higher power. I became more focused on prayer, living by His word, and learning more about the tenants of my faith. The result was that I became more calm and assured in my decision-making and more pleasant to be around.

Again, your endeavors into mind, body, and spirit are personal decisions that I cannot answer for you. However, I do implore you to seek how to make yourself better through these three areas. You will become a better leader as a result.

Have a highly effective time management system, then use it!

The use of a time management system can be an effective and productive strategy. I have famously said, we lead for effectiveness and manage efficiency. The use of a time management system makes us more efficient by focusing on our effectiveness. When we are consistently doing things right, we are not wasting time on mistakes and poor efforts.

I have bounced back and forth many times in the various systems I have employed to become most effective. Time management systems come in a variety of forms. They can be digital, online-based, paper planners, as well as timers and other devices. I have tried many of them. I waned back and forth looking for the best fit for me. Currently, I am back with a paper planner in a leather binder. I am sure many of you are familiar with that product. I am most effective with this style. My best advice is to become familiar with the goal for your system. Some of my colleagues have a secretary or assistant involved in scheduling events and monitoring their email. I do not. This is the reason why

I keep my calendar myself. For me, I am able to align my meetings, plan effectively for the next few days, and provide follow up. Others require a digital method to align their email to their calendar. Again, it is your decision and one that only you can make. However, I will attest to the need to be as organized in your time management as possible.

Know when you should say no. "Prioritize and Execute".

Analogous to time management is the notion of prioritizing your time to be effective. Jocko Willink in his book, *Extreme Ownership* calls it "Prioritize and Execute". When discussing time choices, he means we often face a decision and must choose wisely and quickly. Once a decision or action is made, act firmly and quickly. There is no need to waste time after an action has been selected. In my own use of "Prioritize and Execute", I make sure that my core values are the basis for my decision-making. There is a relationship between the decision and my core values in the speed of execution. The closer in alignment I find my choices and my core values, the quicker I can effectively act. It is when a choice must be made and I find myself not totally aligned with a core value, that I take more time to think. Jocko's point is a clever one; keep the alignment between decisions and values very close.

Intentionally, eat well, move your body, pray, laugh, and smile.

Earlier, we discussed the need for taking care of your mind, body, and spirit. Here, I again emphasize its importance. However, I wish to emphasize that being intentional is the key to success. Anyone can start a diet, begin reading a good book, or even purchase a gym membership. However, being intentional and focused will increase the likelihood that you'll maintain your diet, book, or work out. I'm going to use the dreaded "D" word here to drive the point home. You must, as an effective leader, have a degree of "discipline" to maintain any improvements in your own well being. One of my favorite motivators is David Goggins. He is on Youtube and the other social media sites consistently advocating discipline, hard work, and tenacity. His language is very salty and often offensive. Yet, he connects with my need to hear the truth about quitting and its result. He is blunt and I really need that. I recommend you find a motivator for yourself to help you prioritize and execute your own plan.

Stay off social media. Negativity lives there.

My school and other organizations to which I belong all have a presence on social media. In today's world, we cannot avoid its impact. Social media does have its convenience, yet there are troubling other effects for leaders. While nice to connect with other leaders, we can be scrutinized in yet another forum for opinions and thoughts. You need to be very focused on what reasons you have for maintaining social media accounts. There are many people that have run into negative effects in their workplace as a result of social media. If you are focused and stay disciplined in its use, then social media can serve you well. Just be prepared for the negative posts that online trolls will leave on your school or personal replies to pictures, stories, and posts.

I was personally trolled many times online as a result of an award for our school, a picture sharing a student's success, or even my own posting. Those in the online world have no problem expressing their thoughts about your work. The trouble is that there is no manner for us to share the context of a decision or action. As a leader, I know this is the case, yet I still feel the sting each time it happens. Negativity can take a toll on you. Know what your limits are and how to best manage them.

EXAMPLE

A few years ago, I became too obsessed with my work and became greatly out of balance. I felt justified since I was doing the greater good. It was 80+ hour work weeks, eating dinner on the way to cover athletic events, and not getting enough sleep that wore me down. As I became more and more tired, I was unable to serve as many people as I could. I didn't see it though. It took the Pandemic for me to see that I was living in a state of inertia, or constant movement, and not seeing the effects. I was overweight, stressed out, and short with my loved ones. I looked inward and realized it was my fault and my responsibility to fix it. Lack of balance affected my relationships. I was unhealthy and it started some toxic behaviors. Humility and clarity helped me to get a new plan. A plan to gain balance back in my life, not just during work time.

Lead with Accountability

"You must own everything in your world. There is no one else to blame." Jocko Willink

BOTTOM LINE

You, as a principal, have to own everything in your domain. Principals are whom the "buck stops" within a school. By owning everything, you take responsibility for the effectiveness, or lack thereof, of every facet of your organization. You, as a leader, must hold yourself accountable for the operation of your plan. There is a function of accountability that involves others, however that is not the first place you should look for improvement in your organization. That first glance needs to be in your own mirror. We hold others accountable for their actions as well, however we should start with ourselves. Holding others accountable involves constant feedback, training, and persistence in developing a skill set. Ultimately, if someone fails in your organization, it means that you have failed them. Great leaders model self accountability. They hold themselves accountable. If a problem or challenge arises, leaders should own it. If successes or wins happen, great leaders give them away to their teams. Let your team own a win and celebrate with them. That is the first step on the road to building a deepening culture of excellence.

SUCCESS INDICATORS

Set incredibly high standards for yourself.

Leading an organization requires a tremendous amount of skill, tenacity, and humility. Those are rare characteristics by themselves, let alone as a combination. Probably the most heavily required skill is holding oneself to an incredibly high standard. Great leaders require of themselves what they will not require of others. That sounds atypical. However, managers of the past were very rough on others and required results that they could not meet themselves. That paradigm has changed. What used to be a top-down approach has recently been replaced by a servant-leadership model. To serve others, we must be prepared to do things that we will not ask of others. Serve the organization by serving others.

I remember as a first- year principal, at the end of each day, riding a school bus to the entrance of the parking lot. I would assist buses entering a road with a blind view. It was dangerous and a safety hazard. I was equipped only with a portable stop sign and a smile to stop traffic to let the buses enter the road safely. There is not a chance I would ask anyone else to do that duty. I was the leader and took it upon myself to show the entire organization, bus drivers included, that no one was beyond serving. Yet, I didn't ask anyone else to serve that duty on days where I was not there. I set a standard for myself and that standard was more than I asked of anyone else. Members of our organization still note that gesture of servanthood.

Accept mistakes made by yourself and others as growth opportunities.

Mistakes happen when working with human beings. We are all flawed and not perfect. If you are seeking perfection in others, then leadership may not be the appropriate field for you. However perfect you think you are, there will be times where you miss that standard. Feedback builds skill sets. To grow team members, we must endure mistakes that occur. Growth in leaders often diminishes repeat mistakes. Yet, growth requires friction. I see mistakes that occur as friction along the way to excellence. We need to tolerate and provide support to others who make mistakes along the way to excellence.

Model and share your mistakes.

Humble leaders are a rare commodity. The trait is increasing in great leaders, yet is a low commodity in those considered poor leaders. One way to increase this treasured skill is to admit to your team the mistakes you make as they occur. That is what I call the entry-level for humility. To ascend to the upper levels of humility, and possible greatness, a leader must own the mistakes of their team members and seek to help their members grow. Of course, feedback and learning go hand in hand. To maximize their learning, mistakes must be survivable and not a career death sentence. Of course, there are times when mistakes happen and they have terrible consequences.

Demonstrate what you learned from mistakes.

When we as leaders make mistakes and model learning from them we increase the likelihood that our team members will learn from their mistakes. The inner beauty is that they learn without ever making a mistake. Of course, this requires leaders to fully admit, then debrief our learning and reflections after the mistake has been made. Great leaders possess that much humility.

Show where good happens after mistakes are made.

When you guide inexperienced, aspiring leaders into more sophisticated and capable leaders, they will soak up your teachings about mistakes. Their increasing eagerness to learn will open them up to the possibilities that good can come from these bad instances. Show them the long-term effects on your own learning in reference to a mistake.

EXAMPLE

A few years ago, I made the mortal mistake of accidentally deleting the master schedule. We were in the building phase of a new high school. One of my colleagues was responsible for inputting and constructing the schedule. Nearly 2,000 students' course requests were in the system and the sections for teachers were generated. We were near the end of the schedule building process. I was searching the LMS for staffing numbers and I inadvertently clicked the wrong place and deleted the entire accumulation of data from students and families. That mistake resulted in us having to collect student data from afar and rebuild the schedule in a virtual setting. (Please remember that this was 15 years prior to the world learning how to work in a remote fashion.) As I contacted our new Assistant Principal for scheduling to tell her the bad news, I could sense her anxiety and trepidation. As soon as I got off the phone with her, I called our Chief Technology Officer. He was not happy either. I remember him saying, "Hold on...I'll call you right back." Two hours later, I received a phone call with nearly the entire district office on a conference call. When I looked around and saw the delete happen, my stomach sank. Nevertheless, I owned the mistake, stood tall, and lived through it. I remember taking full responsibility and owning my mistake. It was then I learned complete ownership of mistakes is a great way to establish lasting relationships and build collegiality. A level of trust was established among my team members that I could never replicate. My honesty and humility serve me well to this day. I often share the story and many have commented that they learned from my mistake. My mistake was a big one, yet I survived and many have come to realize that we can falter and not lose our livelihoods. I believe that this safety helped us to be more innovative since leaders were no longer afraid to try new things.

Lead with Confidence

"Never bend your head. Always hold it high. Look the world straight in the eye."

Helen Keller

BOTTOM LINE

Your countenance as a leader will say a lot about you. It will speak volumes about how people perceive you. If you carry yourself in a confident manner, the members of your organization will respond differently to you than if you were to have a meek manner. Please don't mistake my sentiments. I am not saying to carry yourself around in a boastful or bully mentality. Rather, being a confident person will alleviate concerns that others have when they look to you to lead them. Understand that leaders need followers. Those that choose to follow you will only do so if they feel safe and protected. A confident posture will help ensure that feeling for them. Of course, a successful principal's presence is framed by their internal confidence over their own abilities. That foundation speaks loudly to everyone counting on you.

SUCCESS INDICATORS

Display humility and gratitude each day with everyone you meet.

There is a misconception that humble leaders who demonstrate humility must be meek and weak-looking. Nothing could be further from the truth. Humility can be a tenet of confidence when done correctly. Being a leader who demonstrates a calm, humble demeanor resembles confidence more than any arrogant egomaniac. An arrogant egomaniac is rather hectic and not calm. They have an out of control persona about them. I am not implying to rearrange your entire personality. However the skill of acting in a humble, confident manner is intentional.

Analogous to humility is gratitude. These two skills are akin to one another. Displaying gratitude by being pleasant and thankful for the efforts of others is displaying the same attributes that humble people often show. Smiling, being calm, and thankfully reassuring others are features that demonstrate confidence. Similarly, acting in such a manner will build others confidence in your abilities as well.

Know yourself! Be aware of your strengths and weaknesses.

Confident leaders are able to eloquently share their strengths and weaknesses. Strong leaders learn over time what skills they can rely on. Conversely, novice or ineffective leaders may struggle with an accurate depiction of what they can do. They may not have the insight to have employed their range of skills. Perhaps, they are simply listening to their own ego telling them what they wish to hear. Either way, methods of accurate feedback over one's skills is a necessary skill to attain.

Leaders can gain an insight into their abilities if they simply (and humbly) listen to and watch the true results of their decisions and actions. Once insight is gained, it may not be accurate in depiction. Here, trust is invaluable to a leader. They must have a trusted colleague or coach who can guide them in their own feedback loops to be capable of accurately using feedback to assess their abilities. I placed a lot of trust in my closest colleagues on my leadership teams. Often assistant principals were asked exactly how I performed. I would ask very descriptive and objective questions to gain an insight to my own effectiveness. Soon, I was able to develop my own barometer to measure my effectiveness. This barometer became meta-feedback that I could employ to assess my actions and decisions. As I became skilled at using my meta-feedback loop, my confidence rose in situations and with speaking engagements. I was able to make immediate adjustments. This confidence became attractive to aspiring leaders and others on my teams.

Be honest with your own abilities and your team's abilities.

One of the strongest facets of being a confident leader is knowing your strengths and weaknesses. You are fully aware of the strengths and weaknesses of those members of your team. Arrogant leaders think everything is a strength for them, whether it is or not. Arrogance and timidity can be devastating for leaders. Poor leaders put them into situations that they are not appropriately prepared to handle. This is a perfect time to use the Excellence Loop that we discussed earlier. Preparation, practice performance, and process can help build the necessary skills to apply in those situations.

Communicate clearly with a team focus. (We will!)

The most effective leadership and development tool you, as a leader, can employ is to clearly communicate with your team. Stay positive and focused on the objective. Give descriptive and objective feedback in the middle, as well as, at the conclusion. Effective debrief of events and situations are terrific learning opportunities that pay huge dividends. Remember to stay positive and be crystal clear in your expectations prior to action and feedback.

Have consistent courage to do what is hard.

In my many years as a school leader, I have found that courage and confidence are twin sisters. Courtage is the defensive strength in the face of challenges. Confidence is the ability to emerge victorious over these same challenges. Having courage rarely conflicts with being a confident leader. The greater your confidence as a leader, the more apt you are to be able to handle the hard issues and tough situations that arise. Courage is the steel that leaders need in their spine to stand up to the slings and arrows that accompany tough decisions.

EXAMPLE

I remember dealing with a situation involving a staff member. A well-respected and loved teacher was seen in an off-limits area with a female student. Upon investigation, I found that the staff member was involved in an illicit relationship with a student. While it might seem clear cut, doing the investigation and the follow up with the staff member was very difficult. It was a hard situation, yet I had the courage to do what needed to be done. No one could have ever imagined this staff member being involved in anything like that. He was very well liked and respected by so many. I took many slings and arrows from other staff, students, and families alike that simply didn't believe what he was accused of. Albeit, I had to act in the best interest of kids and the organization. Ultimately, he is in prison and the truth came out. Yet, as a leader you are never vindicated. You have to show the confidence to do what is right no matter the cost to you. No one has ever apologized to me or my family for the hurtful and inaccurate statements made and slanderous opinions shared.

Lead with Resilience

"Life doesn't get easier or more forgiving, we get stronger and more resilient."

BOTTOM LINE

Again, Sylvester Stallone famously said, "*It's not how hard you get hit, it's how many times you get back up.*" For school leaders, truer words may have never been uttered. Leaders will take their lumps, have bad days, and terrible disruptions. Do not let your actions or perspective get framed by negativity, hostility, or even mediocrity. Great leaders win despite challenges. They get knocked down but get up each time. Be defined by a good mentality. That is called leadership resilience.

SUCCESS INDICATORS

Share the Jocko Willink philosophy of "Good"

Earlier we discussed Jocko Willink's philosophy. Your team members will jump on board when approaching situations with a "we can do it" mentality. They will be lifted by your countenance as you reply "*Good!... This is our chance to get better!*". It is one of the best stress relievers and confidence builders for your team if you have the resilience to not get distracted by circumstances. Resilience can bring strength to the backbone of your team. They will stand tall in the face of challenge.

Speak with your team about the challenges we all face. "What will we do when it happens?"

Being an open, honest, and transparent leader has many benefits. One of those benefits is the climate of resiliency. Discuss with your team the difficult situations or decisions you are facing. Not only will it bring a stable factor for them to know what's going on, but it is great modeling for their future leadership roles. Your team members will be more apt to remain calm when facing a difficult conversation or an upset parent when they know you are a resilient and confident leader. Modeling sets the tone for them and reinforces your words as a mentor.

When your actions meet your words, is there a congruence and an authenticity?

You develop resiliency when your thoughts or words match your actions. You can talk about enduring a tough situation, but it has to match your actions. When dealing with a tough time, keep a smile on your face, a gleam in your eyes, and a bounce in your step. If you look defeated, those closest to you will see you as defeated. Those that know you best will always have your back. However, as the rest of the staff look to them, it will be obvious to everyone that you are not bouncing back after a setback. Positive alignment of words and actions will confirm your resilience.

Stay positive. Own the difficulties. Avoid gossip.

Of course, you may see a repeating theme developing. When facing difficulties, smile and stay positive. I WILL NOT allow difficult circumstances to beat me. I am a competitive person and no challenges will stop me. No matter the complexity of the circumstance or the size of the challenge faced, I will not be deterred in my pursuit. That relentless effort on the part of a leader, models resiliency that we hope that all kids and staff show. Gossip is one of the most insidious habits that leaders could demonstrate to others. If leaders involve themselves in spreading or sharing gossip, they truly undermine their own effectiveness and leadership. Gossip erodes trust in your leadership and ability to be fair and impartial. As a piece of advice, just don't do it. Losing the trust of your teammates isn't worth it at all.

Win over your troubles.

Successful outcomes show tangible evidence of resilience to everyone in your organization. When in doubt, win over your troubles. Positive attitude, actions, and your own language summarily tell a story to others through your resilience.

EXAMPLE

As a leader, my life can sometimes get in the way. In 2007, my son Will passed away. His passing was a gut punch to me and I still deal with this tragedy to this day. However, I would not let the tragedy affect my life as a leader. I needed to find a way to overcome this in the middle of issues. It became rocket fuel to me as I chose to look at all the kids as my son. I would do for them what I wanted for him. I believe my son, Will, would have wanted me to do that. All of my actions were aligned with what I would do to support my son. Service became therapy for me. I dealt with his loss by extending myself to others. I bounced back.

Lead with Honesty

"Leadership can be defined by one word- honesty. You must be honest with the players and with yourself." Earl Weaver

BOTTOM LINE

Honesty, brutal honesty doesn't need to be harsh. Highly effective leaders need to be honest with others and themselves. When you are clear with your feedback, clear with your directions, and crystal clear with your intentions, members thrive. I use the term "brutal honesty" to mean descriptive, actionable feedback that can be implemented to improve performance. Using the clarifying term "brutal" is not meant to state harsh or hurtful words. It is simply used to mean unambiguous feedback. Too many leaders fall into the trap of using encouragement in place of feedback. Aspiring leaders often give a *"Good Job"* rather than giving a teammate feedback. *"Good Job"* is neither descriptive, nor actionable. Be clear and descriptive. Instead, try *"I really liked the opening to your lesson. It set the tone for what was to be learned and where the learning target would take the class. Well done.*" That example is descriptive, actionable, and can be used to reinforce or improve performance.

SUCCESS INDICATORS

Know your vision so well that you can paint a vivid picture for others.

Great leaders have images in their heads that they seek for their performance and the direction of their organizations. We call these images the vision. That picture should be so well thought out and detailed that you can paint a vivid picture to anyone. The more vivid, the better. Traditionally, the vision is an aspirational look at what we hope our organizations achieve. You, as the leader, should be able to eloquently detail each and every component so well that the listener can enjoy an identical picture. Often we use shortened versions called elevator speeches.

Establish crystal clear lines of communication.

Brutal honesty is clear, unambiguous language. Avoid the use of general terms in feedback situations. Leaders sometimes use "good job" or "well done" to represent feedback on performance. However, that doesn't tell the team member anything that can help with their performance. Clear, honest feedback such as "*I really liked how you opened that conversation...*" gives the person great detailed information on their action that can be replicated. Ultimately, we want others to be able to replicate successful performances and avoid unsuccessful performances.

Find the most "user friendly" times and locations to be honest.

As the leader, you set the conditions for success and provide feedback to everyone in the organization. You are in a position to control when, where, and how you provide honest feedback. Many successful leaders go into a teacher's classroom to provide them feedback that may be taken as critical. It not only puts the teacher more at ease, but it levels the playing field in the power dynamic with you. Providing feedback should not be punitive; it is intended to improve performance. We, as leaders, can control variables to help the teacher receive feedback as purely performance enhancing. Controlling for the location and time is a wonderful step in the right direction. Acknowledging power dynamics can help to ease tensions and improve performance.

Model accepting honest feedback in a civil and dignified way.

As leaders, we are often given people's opinions and feedback about our performance. We must model accepting feedback and criticism in the most leader-like fashion. That means being kind, understanding, and professional when others are giving us their opinions. Often, these opinions can be hurtful and given with negative intentions. Nevertheless, we are the professionals and must act in a professional manner particularly when it is extremely difficult to do so. There are two reasons for this. One, we can de-escalate many situations and emotions when we are calm and professional. If we lose our cool, we have lost control. Two, modeling appropriate actions in tense situations teaches our teammates that professionalism and tact are useful tools. Additionally, our non-reaction can reduce tensions and de-escalate situations quickly.

EXAMPLE

For many years, I have often helped prepare many leaders on my team for Principal and Superintendent interviews. There was a recent leader who I helped to prepare that best illustrates the honest feedback concept. We had worked together for many years and I knew her very well. Her level of expertise was extremely high.

She was a tremendous worker and had great vision. Certainly, she had the chops to be a principal. While a great performer in many areas, I did have to deliver some very honest feedback to her in our preparation sessions. Particularly, feedback about being too verbose in her responses. While incredibly intelligent and a quick thinker, she often would give a multi-paragraphed answer to a simple question. Her answers were incredibly detailed with a lot of follow through information. It was more than any listener could take.

For the next few weeks, I would coach her on shortening her retorts. She took the feedback very well and would attempt to include my guidance. Over time, I saw her improving in general conversation. When she was in a hurry or stressed, the lengthy answers would resurface. Albeit correct, she was losing listeners with her answers. I capitalized on stressful times to reinforce and identified those chances to improve this skill. It took several weeks, but she took the advice and implemented it with fidelity. Now, she is a concise speaker. She is able to blend this skill with her knowledge and work ethic to be an incredible leader. I am truly proud of her and eager to see her career take off.

Lead with Civility

"Try to be the person that no one can out nice." Gary Davison

BOTTOM LINE

Civility is an ethos. Civility is a standard set of behaviors that establish guiding beliefs that organize our actions. In our leadership context, civil actions are the foundation to all of the other behaviors. Without this foundation, our leadership will be met with poor behaviors, selfish interests, and an array of distractions. A leader's character is infinitely more important than their skills.

However, when character and skills are equally present and supported by a culture of civility; then the optimum growth of leaders and organizational excellence can be achieved. This is not an accidental occurrence. Civility is an intentional act that must be attended to constantly. To establish and cultivate trust, others must be able to rely on a leader's actions. Leaders need to plan and execute this action of civil behavior consistently. As regular as they perform any significant function.

SUCCESS INDICATORS

A leader's character is infinitely more important than their skills. People follow people who care.

When a staff member makes a mistake, I need to be quick to support and slow to criticize. Providing feedback is an action of integrity when done with empathy and care. Forgiveness and learning go hand in hand when done empathically and thoroughly. I am often reminded of my grandmother in these times. She often would give me the exact words I needed to learn from a mistake and also know to never do this again. I remember her once telling me that she was "disappointed in me". That memory still gives me chills to this day. That is the last thing I ever wanted to do to her. As a leader I hope to be able to establish a culture to allow for wonderful exchanges when mistakes occur. Her respect was eternal to me. I hope to build that type of commitment in others. I hope to never disappoint these I lead and those I follow.

Actions need to be congruent with the l0ve of others.

Leader's actions are a reflection of a leader's thoughts and beliefs. Civility occurs when character and skills are equally proportioned and aligned with shared goals. Only then, the optimum growth of leaders and organizational excellence can be attained. Those shared goals must be mutually agreed upon and beneficial to all parties. In addition, civility is about trust and caring. A leader needs to act in a manner that is out of care and love for the people they serve. There is a professional obligation to support and serve others, but it goes deeper than that. A great leader is one that acts entirely out of a commitment to the people they serve, not merely professional obligation.

Determine what civility looks like for your organization.

Establishing a norm of civility, is an investment in the operations of a caring organization. There are many times when tough decisions have to be made requiring a level of trust. For example, the Pandemic of 2020 stretched our organization's level of trust in difficult times. During the Spring of 2020, I remember having to tell my staff members "I don't know..." when addressing their questions and concerns. Rather than making up an uncertain answer, I opted for being truthful and relying on my integrity as a leader. Honesty is the best way to answer difficult questions. This level of transparency and honesty is difficult and stress-producing, but the resulting trust builds a culture that will persevere in tough times. Additionally, as a leader invested in growing others, civility is the glue that holds their leadership learning in place. My track record of being honest, as well as showing empathy each day, allows me to be honest with my teams. Criticism stings for everyone. However, when delivered from a trusted source and in an empathetic manner, it is fuel for growth. I have seen more than 20 leaders from our team grow into executive-level leaders in the field of education. This level of honesty and intention toward civility works to grow leaders in all cases.

Make civility a condition for success, not an accidental occurrence.

As a Principal, I am often asked what my job entails. To be clear, I tell others that my primary responsibility is to set the conditions for success and provide feedback to others. In setting conditions for the organization and all members to be successful, many skills need attention. Such skills are: understanding what others say, listening to the needs of others, leading with kindness, being loyal and appreciating the loyalty of others, seeking to protect & serve others in difficult times, acting with integrity and truthfulness, having an appropriate vision for the organization, alignment of personal and organizational needs, seek "common success" together, empowering others, and seeking comfort in a time of risk-taking. Of course, different settings bring different sets of characteristics to play.

This culture is possible when the intentional focus is effectiveness rather than efficiency. People will often wait patiently for excellence when they know it is a possibility. However, they will remain impatient when the focus is on efficiency and they receive low quality results. Subsequently, setting the conditions for civility and success are able to go hand-in-hand together. An effective culture is poised to pursue excellence.

EXAMPLE

In 2006, I was named Principal of a neighboring high school. It had a tremendous track record of academic success. It was seen by the outside world as the crown jewel of the school system. During the Spring of 2006, I was transitioning in to relieve the current Principal. He was leaving to open a new high school the following school year. This afforded me time to meet with the staff, introduce myself to others, and learn about their traditions, culture, and systems. One such opportunity was a Spring Leadership Team meeting. This bi-monthly meeting was populated by their administrative team and department chairs, as well as crucial support staff. Coming into the meeting, I assumed that their culture of success was deep on collegiality, respect, and civility. This could not be further from the truth. The purpose of this meeting was to discuss and set in place new priorities for a grading and reporting policy to be used the next school year.

My chagrin was evident as the meeting opened. The current principal, Ralph, greeted them with a barrage of statements. He gave them "talking points" he wanted them to know. These "talking points", or demands, were his negative expectations and anticipated results he desired. Basically, he fed them a prescription of the desired outcomes he wanted without their participation. It was obvious to me, as an outsider, that he intended this meeting to take only a few minutes. He told me prior to the meeting as he wished to "prepare" me for meeting the team. His tone was dictatorial, his voice level was loud and disruptive and set the negative tone. Several members of the Leadership Team followed his lead. For example, the Mathematics Department Chairperson, Leslie, refused to be open to any collegial discussion as she told the room, "We in the math department are NOT doing any of this stuff." She was cheered on by Ricky, the Career Tech Department Chairperson. He was acting childishly and voicing sarcastic comments at every opportunity. He rolled his eyes, made jokes, and high-fived Leslie. The two were not friends yet, but were bonded together by their inappropriate behavior.

Lauren, the eager Assistant Principal, tried to get the meeting back on track by describing the changes needed in upcoming grading policy. However, her efforts were thwarted by PE Department Chair, Roland. He read headlines from a newspaper aloud. His point was well-made as it was evident that he was not going to engage in any discussion of change. Additionally, he flagrantly rattled the newspaper each time the pages were turned. Lauren became frustrated and attempted to chastise him. She indicated that he was "not important" in the effort to change a grading policy since he was incapable of giving "appropriate grades" in PE classes. As Roland rose from his chair to leave, he loudly yawned and was met by Lauren's next belittling statement.

"Do you even need to be in here?" she said with the sarcasm that Ricky enjoyed. Even though Physical Education wasn't considered a "core subject", PE was a department consisting of 12 teachers who gave performance assessments to athletes and students. Their input could be substantial in the effort toward this change in grading policy. They could be a resource for other departments as this change would subsequently affect everyone. Their knowledge and experience could be vital as professional learning should have been discussed…but never was.

After the back and forth spanned into the 15th minute, the English Department Chair, William, began to ask questions indicating that he was seeking more information. His desire to gain understanding was met by Lauren telling him "You just need to do what we tell you." He raised his eyebrows, sat back in his chair, lowered his head, closed his notebook, and was silenced for the remainder of the meeting. Principal Ralph took no opportunity to get the meeting back on track. He did not seem very interested in anything but his freshly-pressed suit that was getting wrinkled by sitting in a library chair. His attitude was clear. Ralph was more than content with this behavior as it reflected his own attitude toward the staff. There was a firm culture in place, yet it was not what I expected.

The example I submit to you is a true story. Names of staff are changed, yet the behaviors are real. The school was high-achieving and took pride in their students' abilities. There were tremendous teachers and highly dedicated staff all wanting the very best for kids. Yet, the culture was aligned in the wrong direction. It was very much a top-down mentality. In a few months, I entered as their next Principal. Over time, I further understood that this example was a learned behavior. Civility had to be a staff expectation. We were a large organization and very disjointed by the geography of the buildings. There were three distinct and separate campuses on a large piece of property. The job at hand was very similar to "turning the Titanic in rough waters". Yet, it had to be done. This change was evident to many leaders in the system. Building a culture of collegiality, empowerment, and trust had to be established to start long-term improvement. Again, as a learning organization, they were not broken. If you look at their yearly testing results, they were one of the best schools in the state. However, what level of performance could they have attained had their philosophy and culture matched? Their leader was not interested in pushing beyond being pleased and satisfied. He was comfortable with the comfort of satisfaction, setting a poor example, and tolerating poor behaviors.

Lead by Joy

"The measure of a leader is not the number of people who serve them but the number of people he serves." John Maxwell

BOTTOM LINE

RELIGIOUS BELIEFS ALERT I believe that a leader's personal beliefs can greatly affect their effectiveness. It has been said that JOY means Jesus, Others, Yourself. This has set a tone for my priorities as a person and as a leader. These beliefs certainly affect how I choose to serve others. A higher power has helped me to serve their "work" but I looked at them as people, not employees. Jesus has given grace and forgiveness in my life. Through this gift, I am encouraged to do the same for those I serve. Leadership is clearly about serving others; service without expecting anything in return.

SUCCESS INDICATORS

Assess "Why?" you serve.

Service is about what you can do for others in your organization. When you are interjected as a leader, you have a drive to excel. That drive is based upon your internal motivation. That motivation is what keeps you going through long hours, upset people, difficult situations, and tumultuous times. Motivation has a fuel source. That source is called your "why?" Your "why?" is part motivator, part belief system, and part moral barometer. It keeps you going when the tough need to keep going. Identify your why and use it each day as a baseline for your decisions, actions, and leadership philosophy. Your "why?" is a cumulation of your core beliefs.

Intentionally serve others before yourself.

I read a great book by Simon Sinek (2017) called "Leaders Eat Last". In that book, Sinek brings home the point that leaders are put here to serve, not be served. I, wholeheartedly, agree with his sentiment. Although, I'd like to go a step further. Not only are leaders given the privilege of serving them. Leaders are given the privilege to commit fully to the organization as a whole. Not only do individuals get our attention, the sum of the organization does too. He implies this, but our first obligation is to the organization. By serving the entity, we are serving all the individuals within the entity.

Smile with the gratitude of a believer in what you're doing.

As a believer, I can say that my beliefs have taught me to turn the other cheek and smile. That is an easy task when things are good and situations are at ease. However, when your team is in crisis or you are dealing with a difficult situation, smiling may be tough or even impossible. That's where toughness and joy intersect. Demonstrating joy in the midst of terrible circumstances is the true measure of your beliefs in action.

I remember once when a student who dropped out waited on me at a fast food restaurant. He cursed, shrugged, then spit in my face. Anger, despair, and intoxicating substances ruled his life. He had lost his way. I do remember him in better times. He was funny, incredibly intelligent, and very quick-witted. I really liked that kid. What I found today was a shell of that young man. However, I could not react to the behavior as that is not the core of this kid. After I wiped my face, I shook my head and told him it was good to see him and I wished he'd stop by school so we could talk one day. Smiling the entire time, I never broke into anything close to anger or judgment. That seemed to completely catch him off guard. He expected a certain reaction. Rather, he was confused and just walked away. My intention was to plant a seed with him. I was eager to show him that the world was not the place he saw when he opened his eyes. Maybe one day, that seed will grow into a tree that will shade him from the rains that he is expecting.

You can only serve yourself AFTER you serve others.

Leading in joy does not mean that we disregard or ignore our own needs. We are not to forget to serve ourselves. Rather, we are to meet our needs after we meet the needs of the people we are charged with serving. This may sound antithetical to leading with balance. To a certain degree, it can run contrary. However, when we budget time, resources, and our attention properly, we can meet their needs. Then, we move on to our own needs. Intentionality means that we fundamentally focus on supporting those around us. Also, keeping our needs on that spectrum as well.

EXAMPLE

One day we had a staff luncheon after an early release day. My leadership team took care of the student's dismissal. This made it possible for all the staff to go eat first prior to us coming into the cafeteria. It was a tremendously rainy day. Dripping wet and cold from rain, our team came into the building to join the staff. Unfortunately, one member of my team took advantage of the short line and went to eat before anyone else. I find this extremely distasteful from a leadership perspective. We are here to serve, and not be served. After the meal and meeting, I had a conversation with him. At first, he appeared to learn from the feedback that I provided. To my chagrin, he did not. In the 13 years since that incident, he has not progressed in his leadership journey. Rather, he seems to have defined himself as a leader who is in the role for himself. It is truly unfortunate as I find him to be very skilled in many areas of leadership, but he cannot commit to the character needed to serve others first. This is an indication that leaders must have a complete package of skills to be fully prepared to lead an organization.

Lead by Personal Brand

"All of us need to understand the importance of branding. We are CEOs of our own companies: Me Inc." Tom Peters

BOTTOM LINE

Personal branding is the process of creating an identity for yourself as an individual. This involves developing a well-defined and consistent look, message, and presence online and offline. There are many psychology-based reasons why you might want to work on your personal brand. Successful principals and great leaders can establish solid cultures within their organizations with an effective personal brand. Students and staff know who to follow based on what you stand for. Personal brand is not meant to indicate that we are advocating for being egocentric in your organization. Rather, it is about the alignment of your beliefs and actions to the mission of your organization. When the two are aligned, the congruence brings faith in the mission and depth to your leadership intentions. Comfort, in this context, indicates trust and stability. Members of organizations are ripe to flourish in these contexts. This is the recipe for organizational success.

SUCCESS INDICATORS

Clearly define and "publicize" what your core values are.

Core values are the heart of your decision-making and culture-building actions. They are the most closely held beliefs you have. Core values are those beliefs you are willing to quit over. Obviously, we are not talking about anything criminal or unethical, rather they are the beliefs that are what make you…you. They are the most obvious things people would say about you. Even though many people who know you well might be able to identify your core values, you need to make them obvious to anyone who pays any attention to you. As a leader, there will be many eyes on you. What that being said, make certain that those eyes are watching your beliefs as they see you.

Align your actions to your values.

As a leader there will be many eyes on you. Your every action should be aligned with what it is that you hold most closely to you. Each step in your actions should be in clear alignment with what you believe. For example, if a core belief is that students with disabilities will get the best opportunities to grow in your school, your actions must represent that belief. You shouldn't locate the special education classes in trailers near the back of your campus. You should be visible in their classes, encourage them as a priority, and develop a master schedule with them in mind. This attention will make it even more obvious what you believe as the leader.

Articulate your "why" as you make decisions.

Once your beliefs are obvious to those around you, it is important to share and demonstrate why you believe this is important to your organization. This understanding will give a context to others to know and be able to accommodate your priorities. Understanding beliefs is the first step to replicating them.

47

Once this action step is "bone deep" in your culture, your beliefs will be ingrained into your organization. For example, I was a student who struggled in high school. I truly understand those kids who do not excel. Thus, student support has been a core value of mine in each school I lead. I cannot only sympathize with them, but I can understand their struggles. I know the way a school can make them feel when they are not a priority. The rest of the organization now values student support as a core tenet of our school. My actions clearly and intentionally articulate my beliefs about kids, academic support, and the culture.

Be consistent to your core values at all times.

Consistency is a critical feature of core values if you want them to be replicated. It's easy to stand firm on your beliefs in good times. When facing a challenge can you, as the leader, continue to stand on your beliefs when they are not understood or popular? I posit that it is even more important to do so in tough times. You, as a leader, will gain trust and respect by being consistent and firm in your beliefs.

For example, each year, we develop a master schedule with many priorities in mind. However, the core value of student support is a critical one that must not be overlooked. To that end, we built our entire bell schedule and master schedule around the notion of a one-hour block for all kids to have in the middle of the day. That block allows for our kids to access supports at all levels of academic challenge. This is an example of putting my core values into action. It is disruptive to carry out some days, arduous to plan for in the spring, and difficult to keep up with on a daily basis. However, the benefit for kids, academically, has been tremendous. It is more work, but we all agree that the effort is worth the sacrifice.

All of the schools I have led, all had the same foundation of core beliefs. They were based on high student and staff spirit, a committed energy, very high student support procedures, a high degree of autonomy for teachers, a high use of feedback, and low tolerance for selfishness. These tenets were not only shared among the staff and community when I started at each school; they were my actions at all times. The staff and community saw an alignment that was so congruent that there were no surprises. Positive alignment between beliefs and actions breeds confidence in the leader and the organization. After beginning at each school, I then started to introduce and deepen the beliefs that I treasured. It started with my conversation, then my actions, then the planning for the organization, and finally the actions of the organization were aligned to those beliefs. It took several years to get them aligned. As a leader, you are playing the long game.

Lead through Fairness

"Treating others with fairness and dignity is the rain and sun that helps others grow." Gary Davison

BOTTOM LINE

Principals may be familiar with the following maxim: *"Fair is not equal and equal is not fair"*. This is only true when you lead by your core values, head toward a solid vision, and effectively communicate. "Fair" and "equal" are terms that are misconstrued in today's world. Fair is giving someone what they need to have the opportunity to be successful. Equal is giving everyone the same amount. Please don't get me wrong, this is not a political issue. In recent years, it has been made into a political issue by many. In my terms, how we treat people is not political. It is more important than that. It is an aspirational goal to be achieved by the best of us to treat all people well. Equal is a synonymous term to teachers, students, and parents but leaders often see the difference between equal and fair. When treating people equally, we are assuming they need the same things to be successful. By treating people fairly, we are giving people exactly what they require to have the opportunity to be successful. Obviously, we cannot guarantee everyone success, but we must aspire for all to have the opportunity for success. Predictive outcomes are never at play in the field of leadership, but we, as school leaders, can aspire for all kids to be treated fairly in the pursuit of opportunities.

SUCCESS INDICATORS

Constantly model "Fair isn't equal, and equal isn't fair" by prioritizing these growing trends.

As leaders, we are often asked to make choices when budgeting, planning, disciplining, preparing, and executing goals and plans. The maxim, *"fair isn't equal and equal isn't fair"*, is heard in some schools across America. However, is it really being adhered to? For example, when schools budget, principals often give equal amounts to departments across the school. I understand why these principals do this. But does it really meet the goal of fairness? Not really. Fairness means that the special education department may need more funds to offset the lack of progress their kids are making. Similarly, the AP (Advanced Placement) program may not need as many funds as the ESOL (English as a Second Language) department based upon academic priorities. Fairness means that we treat everyone based upon their needs. Equal, however, means that everyone gets the same treatment no matter what needs are present.

Plan for fairness.

Fairness is an aspirational goal that I seek every day. The fear of many leaders is that if you do something for one and not all then you are "setting a precedent". I am so sorry to dispel this notion, but learning is not a clean progression for all people. It might take me longer to learn an equation than you. I need more repetition or practice doesn't mean that I should not have the opportunity to learn. Fairness means that things will not look identical from one person to another. A great leader must be comfortable with that notion. You must be able to articulate and understand the differences between being equal to each other and being fair to one another. To be able to execute fairness properly, a great leader must plan for fairness. Be open to arrangements and alternate plans for the kids who may require more to learn. Be ready for the naysayers who might ask you about it.

Make your budget and time schedules based upon the "Fairness" doctrine.

A doctrine is the codification of a set of beliefs. Making fairness a doctrine is an easy action for a leader. Simply, use fairness for ALL kids as a filter that all decisions run through. When establishing a budget, do budget priorities and then align the budget based upon priorities. Do the same process with building a master schedule. What are the critical factors some of your kids need? Using this priority-building structure is a great way to justify your time or financial expenditures and makes you accountable to the instructional outcomes of your school.

EXAMPLE

Over the last ten years, I have learned to assign my time to this maxim. As I grow leaders and lead the organization, there are members of my team and the staff that need more of my time than others. For example, a new yearbook advisor is learning the processes of a $400,000 entity, while still teaching English classes within the school day. The additional stress of running a major financial entity in our school is daunting. To this end, I am available to her whenever she needs guidance. The same is true of a veteran teacher, who is new to our school. He probably will not need as much guidance and prompting. If not, I don't want to bother him. Conversely, a new teacher to the profession and our school will need more of my time. I am always happy to prioritize my time to those who need it. Those who need more of my time deserve me spending it there. It is not a slight to anyone else, but those who require more of my time will get it. Prior to each week, establish time priorities and intentionally schedule them in your calendar.

Lead with Humility

"Humility shows great strength. The uninitiated see weakness. It is the strongest leaders who admit mistakes and fix them." Gary Davison

BOTTOM LINE

Humility is not being saddled with the burden of an overabundance of pride or arrogance. In today's leadership world, humility is seen as a necessary skill to be able to cultivate culture in organizations. Principals who practice humility develop more followers, high collaboration, and high student achievement; all through a better school culture. Humility is recognized as an incredible super power to the initiated. Those that do not know, see humility as a sign of weakness. Jim Collins (2001), author of Good to Great, found two common traits of CEOs in companies that transitioned from average to superior market performance: humility being chief among them. Humility is an ability that is a predeterminer of success in organizations.

SUCCESS INDICATORS

Seek and listen to the contributions of others.

As stated before, humility is the lack of pride or arrogance. To be humble, listening is a predominant action. As important as it is to listen, knowing that your leader wants to listen to you and then actually does, builds trust. This indicator of success has several steps to it. One, the leader must be willing to listen to others. Two, the leader should actually do so. Third, the leader must put others in a position to give their opinions. Finally, the leader must value and put some of those suggestions into effect. Notice there is not a choice whether to put suggestions into place. You, as the leader, can choose which to emphasize.

Be grateful & show gratitude to everyone. Especially to those who oppose you.

Humility is not simply being quiet and letting others talk. Humility is being happy to include others in the process of discussion and being thankful for their involvement and input. Being humble is not an exclusive position for those who simply agree with you. Humility can be a more important tool to those who oppose your opinions. I agree that there are times to stand up for your thoughts, beliefs, and opinions; however, defending those in a humble manner can strengthen your argument. For example, I proposed a new structure for student support. This new system would involve many staff members restructuring their time within the school day. It was an imposition and moved a lot of people's cheese. It was not very popular at first. No one ever really wants to go through a monumental shift or change. This was to be a very large change, both philosophically and structurally. Yet, I used humility in speaking with those that opposed my vision for student support and included the most vocal detractors in the process. This level of embracing humility won them over and we actually ended up with a better version. I attribute their involvement in the process as the reason the result was better than I had envisioned.

Openly admit mistakes, be proud of them, fix them.

Leading with humility means not hiding your mistakes, warts, and other goofs. We, as leaders, will make mistakes. Leaders not showing or hiding their mistakes doesn't allow their teams to see that they are actually human. Trust is built by leaders who are being transparent with their mistakes. When trust is built, team members will build a collegial culture of learning among members of their team. I have famously shared my mistakes and goofs to anyone on my teams and staff. I like to lead in a "flat" leadership structure (see FLAT Leadership at the end of this chapter). It is very consistent with leading in a humble fashion. The two philosophies work hand in hand to compliment one another.

Ask for help gladly when you need it.

Leaders are only in a position of authority because someone helped them in their leadership journeys. We have relied on others at many times in our path to the principalship. Once in a position, some leaders feel that they should not ask for assistance any longer. There is nothing further from the truth. No principal can be an expert in every area that they need to have knowledge. I rely on the expertise of others every day. Often I reach out to those on my own as I am not the most knowledgeable person. If I have a question about a chemistry class, I cannot effectively answer that question. Thus, I ask one of our very talented chemistry teachers. They are much more knowledgeable than I am. I hope to honor their expertise by reaching out to them for their assistance. My expertise lies in the areas of organizational leadership and management. I know my lane and stay in it. However, my lane includes humility enough to be able to reach outside my lane to inquire with those whose lane I do not share.

Humble leaders are not exempt from making additional mistakes. My mistakes are often ones of congruence and alignment. I hope to stay consistent with my actions and words. If my actions show arrogance, but my words are humble; I am not in agreement. However, if my words and actions are aligned then my humility is more likely to be trusted and our culture will benefit. Passion, tempers, and unintentional words are the most common offenders of incongruence.

EXAMPLE

Early in my career as a principal, I was making a schedule that I thought would benefit the teachers at the kindergarten grade level. I hoped it would save them time to be able to plan together. However, it was not taken well by the team of teachers on the grade level. I stood up at a faculty meeting and shared my plan. To my chagrin, it went over like a lead balloon. I was dumbfounded. No one would say anything. I suppose that I expected applause and adulation, however it was more like a room full of crickets. However disconcerting, I moved on to the next topic. Later in the day, a trusted teacher on the grade level came and shared that the team of teachers did not like the plan. Apparently, they felt it was overreaching to establish such a plan. I had to agree since I hadn't even noticed hearing that there was ever a problem. I tried to "fix" something that was not broken. Imagine the arrogance I displayed imagining there was a problem when one did not exist. I had to come clean with the entire staff. I did at the next faculty meeting and the process of being humble to them went a long way to earning their trust. I remember this story to this day and use it often to remember that I am only a member of the staff, not any more important than anyone else on the team. I simply serve a different role than others do. We each serve in various capacities to the benefit of the organization. Leaders need to remember this!

RESOURCES: FLAT Leadership

Quote: *"Leadership is not about titles, positions, or flow charts. It is about one life influencing another."* John C. Maxwell

Being a leader means that others are willing to commit to your ideas… That is a rather simple concept. One person (or group) leads, decides, acts, prompts, selects. At its most basic element, leading convinces another to agree to act in a certain manner or to complete a specified act. This implies a hierarchy of some sort. A positional power relationship is naturally a result. In this writing I am rebuffing the notion of one person leading from a basis of power. I realize that a power component is always present when the buck stops on one person's desk, however one does not have to rely on this dynamic to lead others. FLAT leadership is a concept that I have used to accomplish two fundamental tasks: One, I was tasked by my first Superintendent to grow more leaders for our school system. Two, establish a culture of shared leadership to enhance a collaborative environment. I did not begin my administrative career with the vision of FLAT leadership, rather it developed as I attempted to accomplish these two facets. Ultimately, I feel that my organizations have benefited greatly from the use of FLAT leadership.

Compare and contrast two endings of a scenario…

Scenario:

Today is a fine Fall Monday morning. There are ten people sitting around a conference room table. The four women and six men are of various positions and ranks. It is a regularly scheduled administrative leadership meeting. They are leading a large suburban high school in a Southeastern state. The table is long, made of cherry wood, and pointed toward a large computer board used for projection. Around this table, laptop computers and tablets are used by each member to take notes and research answers for questions being raised. Davis, the school principal, opens the meeting by reviewing the agenda and setting purpose for the meeting.

What follows are two examples of how this meeting might transpire.

One : After setting the purpose of the meeting, Davis now introduces topics on the agenda. The agenda has been aligned with members' strengths of the team and sets the stage for them to guide the discussion. The discussion goes back and forth in a respectful participatory manner among all at the table. Laughing, smiling, raised brows, and nodding are reflecting the hospitable tone of the day. The discussion and chatter are evidence that all are members on topic and participating. Tim, an affable Assistant Principal, begins to discuss his plans for a school pep rally and a follow up spirit project. It will take a couple of weeks to organize and many hands to execute. Nevertheless, he introduces the timeline, certain aspects that affect everyone, and asks questions about the details of the overall schedule to see if it fits the plan. Dru, the pleasant Athletic Director, gives Tim some feedback that resonates as wise. Additionally, Dru gives Tim some good-natured joking about his project. Tim appreciates his words and thanks him for the thoughts. There appears to be an overlap in events that may affect the execution of the pep rally and spirit event. Ross, another Assistant Principal, announces that there are standardized testing events that will prohibit several students from attending as well. Tim now asks if there are alternate dates/times that can be selected. Andy, a well-liked Dean of Students announces that he has anticipated this and has a backup date in mind. "A week later" he announced. "It still honors the teams and kids we want to celebrate." Nodding of heads and chatter of agreement indicate that Andy saved them all from certain disaster. Tim reinforces that he and his team will make it work. The entire team agrees that the new date is a great option. The meeting continues on to the next topic.

Two: After setting the purpose of the meeting, Davis now introduces the topics on the agenda. He gives a full and robust explanation of what he is seeking with each and every agenda item. He is thorough and committed to detail. Each member of the team listens attentively for the details that mirror their assigned duties. If there are items that pertain to their assigned duties, then they ask clarifying questions. They look to handle their responsibilities to the standard Davis describes. Autonomy and choice are non-existent for them as the standard is set by Davis and his vision. Each member is cordial and congenial to one another. However each member is assigned tasks that reflect their predetermined duties, their reliability, and their capacity. The discussion is led by Davis and the conversation does not stray from the topic. All members are on task and side conversations are kept at a minimum. Davis asks Tim if the pep rally is planned and ready to go. "Yes, sir" replies Tim as he keeps his head down. There appeared to be something that needed to be stated. All of the members are looking down…no words are spoken…silence. "Any discussion?" asks Davis. Crickets could have been heard around the table. "I guess that we are good then.." With that Davis moves on to the next topic on the agenda.

The examples are quite extreme, yet serve as contrast to the types of leaders that I have encountered. Which are you? Do you see yourself in either example? Davis (in the first example) uses FLAT leadership to manage tasks, develop leadership in others, and prepare for possible incongruent actions that can affect the best laid plans.

FLAT leadership has four fundamental facets. Below are the elements:

F- Foundational

"Do what is right, not what is easy." Unknown

Foundational- A leader does not need to be the smartest person in the room. Ideally, they would have a level of acumen regarding the field they are leading outside... However, I have found it best to be confident in my abilities yet able to rely on those who are superior in their knowledge of the field. Organizations need leaders that understand and adhere to the simplest, most foundational aspects that constitute success in their field. For example, as a high school principal, the foundational needs we need are: communicating clearly to students and families, organizing resources, remaining current on instructional pedagogy, and maintaining a calm, kind demeanor. Foundationally, the leader of a school is not an expert in any one field, yet an expert in many fields. This simply is not possible for every principal to be an expert in content areas science, mathematics, social science fields, and all languages), instructional pedagogy, safety & security, finances, transportation, athletics, all extra-curricular areas, and everything else. Thus, leaders need to be able to rely on the expertise of others. I task myself with daily work to accomplish two areas: I set the conditions of success for my colleagues and I provide them feedback toward those conditions.

L- Leadership Lessons...

"Leadership develops daily, not in a day." John Maxwell

FLAT leadership is a tool I have used for many years to grow leaders in strong, capable leaders of their own organizations. One major element has been to share and discuss "leadership lessons" with each member. Aspiring leaders need experience with difficult, stressful, and arduous situations to develop the instinctual fortitude to be able to handle situations. When a leader embraces the difficulty within a stressful event, members of the team feel confidence in their ability and thus are more effective in their actions. However, to develop this capacity in aspiring leaders, I cannot place them into situations when they are unprepared. The more effective manner I have used to develop capacity is to verbalize my thinking within the midst of a situation and debrief with aspiring leaders at the conclusion of the event. Additionally, I use past experiences that are synonymous to events currently taking place. This base of knowledge provides aspiring leaders with the slight experience (albeit through my experience) to build a framework of confidence. Below is an example of a "Leadership Lesson" I recently used with a colleague.

LL- The situation is that a young administrator encounters an upset student who has a difficult time cooling off after a confrontation with a teacher. The student feels they were blamed for cheating on a test when their cell phone rang. The administrator needed to ascertain the details. What would you do next and what do you do to resolve so that both feel they can move forward? This is a very common type of encounter that school administrators deal with on a daily basis. It is rather rudimentary, yet fundamental for an aspiring school leader. One misstep and a relationship between the student and teacher could be lost. One also runs the risk of a volatile parent confrontation. Once the scenario is shared, I discuss all of the options with the aspiring leader. I hope for them to talk more than me… I can only really determine their capacity as I sense their honesty. As they grow in their leadership abilities, I then place them in actual scenarios that are somewhat similar to ones we enacted in our "Leadership Lessons" discussions.

A- Actionable Feedback

"An ounce of action is worth a ton of theory." Ralph Waldo Emerson

As the leader I "set the conditions for success" and then provide feedback based upon performance. I consider feedback to be the fuel for all performance...good performance or bad performance. If your team experiences poor performance, look directly at the amount, timing, and type of feedback given to members of the team performing poorly. It's been my experience that limited or non-existant feedback lead directly to lackluster results. I visualize a compass when thinking of feedback. On one end (call it East) is the extreme where no feedback is given. There you have a laissez faire, "let them be" attitude. Many leaders live here thinking that if they guide their members by providing feedback they are "micromanaging". Let's call this end of the compass the East end zone. On the West end of the compass you have a very non-laissez faire, type A, hovering with a focus on direct, explicit feedback. This end details every move a member should take each and every moment... As with many things, there is a happy balance that I believe brings the best results. Of course, feedback is critical, but a member being able to utilize feedback to amend or guide their subsequent performance is optimum. Let me illustrate my point. I cannot imagine Coach Nick Saban of the Alabama Crimson Tide football team allowing a new offensive tackle to perform a block inaccurately in practice without receiving feedback to improve his performance. Additionally, he will not wait until the day of the game to give the feedback necessary to improve his results. Alternatively, Coach Saban will not detail out each and every component for the OT in excruciating detail every time he misses a block. The OT is expected to learn from the feedback to achieve the maximum result. See, feedback is critical in the learning cycle.

T- Treat them Fair...

"Fairness does not mean everyone gets the same. Fairness means everyone gets what they need." Rick Riordan

Leaders treat colleagues fairly by serving WITH them and not expecting others to serve them. The image I always hold is the leader serving shoulder to shoulder with the members of their organization. One book I ask members of my leadership teams to read is *"Leaders Eat Last"* by Simon Sinek. Understanding your place in the organization as a leader, sets the dynamic of fairness for all members in the organization. Ideally, if I, as a school principal, attend to daily hallway duty, stand in for a teacher who has an obligation, and kindly set the conditions for the organization to attain success. By "setting conditions" I mean that leaders define expectations for the movement of the organization. They do not set the expectations, rather the leader assists members of the group to organize toward their efforts. It is the task of the leader to guarantee the equality and fairness of the opportunity for members of the organization. The adherence to the strategic plan and effectiveness of the members guarantee the validity of the outcome.

"Perfection is not attainable, but if we chase perfection we can catch excellence."

Vince Lombardi

FLAT leadership has, to date, helped me to develop 19 leaders that have gone to lead their own schools and school systems. It is certainly not perfect, but has guided me to develop capacity within a very large high school. I am thankful to the many leaders that have helped me to develop this style.

Lead by Kindness/Caring

"Constant kindness can accomplish much. As the sun makes the ice melt, kindness causes misunderstanding, mistrust, and hostility to evaporate." Albert Schweitzer

BOTTOM LINE

As a principal, your positive, smiling demeanor can start the most difficult of circumstances on a good foot. Follow through with calm, upbeat words and actions can effectively start the process of excellence toward goals. Kindness is the first tool that a leader can employ to show respect, a positive culture, and true openness to anyone in their organization. Kindness is a key, fundamental skill that cannot be overlooked or taken for granted.

SUCCESS INDICATORS

Kindness is currency that allows for open dialogue.

In the movie, "Roadhouse", Dalton (played by Patrick Swayze) was the main character. He rides into town as a grizzled bar bouncer. Soon, he is subjected to many instances of people wanting to challenge him physically. When training the new staff of bouncers at the Double Deuce, a fictional bar in which he works, he proclaims to the group that his main strategy to deal with drunks and obnoxious bar goers is to "Be Nice". This doesn't go over very well with a team dealing with a rough crowd. His philosophy wins out in the end and the town has new respect for his talents. Obviously, fictional movies are unique in the way they use various approaches to solve problems. However, I cannot disagree with what Dalton proclaims in the movie. Being nice is a great first step to allow others to understand your perspective and de-escalate when you need to have open dialogue. I often challenge myself to "outnice" someone else. Creating a game out of it challenges me to always be intentional to everyone I meet.

Actions are the visible expressions of kindness.

Not only speaking in a kind tone helps resolve difficult situations, your actions can serve to build trust in your words. Unfortunately, there are some who are distrustful of a leader that is armed with a kind disposition. They may have been treated horribly after kind words have been shared with them. They are distrustful of leaders and are wounded. I find this too often when dealing with new teachers and new veteran staff. Smiling, opening doors for people, giving a helping hand when possible, and asking people about their interests and families reinforces a kind approach. When those words and actions are paired, trust is due to develop your relationship into one that is balanced, kind, and collegial.

A kind attitude is the baseline for the culture of your organization.

A school culture that supports kindness begins with the leader. The actions and words of the leader establish the expectations for behavior in an organization. Team members will follow the actions of a respected leader. The norms established are a visible example of the core values of the leader and the organization. Developing a kind, people-centered organization takes time, focus, established norms, and feedback. Culture begins with the leader and their actions.

Timing is critical.

An effective leader takes every opportunity to act intentionally toward setting positive actions toward the organizational goals and norms. Each time a kind gesture is extended, the leader has an opportunity to encourage further kindness and replication of positive actions. The closer the encouragement is given to the action, the more likely it is to be replicated and reinforced. Members should be encouraged as close to the actions leaders wish to see.

EXAMPLE

As a leader, your actions and words are critical to ensuring the trust built as an organization. Each morning, I stand at the intersection of the three main entrances to our school. The auditorium entrance welcomes all of the bus riders. The main entrance welcomes the car riders. The gym entrance welcomes the students that drive themselves. This intersection is the crossroads of all students moving throughout the building. This is a location where I can be highly visible and interact with many students and staff. I interact with hundreds of students each day by smiling, saying "Good Morning", as well as, having conversations with kids. There are four doors that open to the courtyard in the middle of the building. I often hold the doors open for kids entering and exiting from the courtyard. My goal each morning is to interact with as many students as I can. This interaction is intended to set a tone of kindness in our building with kids each day. The result has been that I have exceedingly good relationships with many students that I would never have interacted with.

Lead with Personal Integrity

"Own the bad and give away the good..." Gary Davison

BOTTOM LINE

As a Principal, others put us on a pedestal or give us undeserved prestige. The traditional view of a school principal is that we sit in an office, drink coffee, wait for the phone to ring, and ask our secretary to take a message. I often think of Mr. Belding in the television show "Saved By The Bell" as the traditional depiction of a high school principal. In reality the job of the principal is an unending series of issues, tasks, uncertain outcomes to unwavering situations, and many circumstances we are not trained to handle. Great principals handle all of these ambiguous situations with a hardy "whatever it takes" attitude. There is a degree of fact to that. However, personal integrity leads to being a stoic, reliable leader who is ready to build trust.

SUCCESS INDICATORS

Be the leader that says what you mean, and mean what you say!

Integrity means to be congruent with our actions and words. As a leader, your words carry a lot of weight to many people. The opinions you can shape with those words can help or hinder your organization's culture in the blink of an eye. Be understanding that your words have the power to lift someone up and make their day better. By contrast, your words can tear someone down and put them into shambles. When you go to share your words or give feedback, understand that those words are taken by many and replayed in their heads over and over again. Be careful with your word choice, as well as your tone. Both have the ability to define your meaning without you ever selecting such. A great leader is careful with their words. They are also congruent that their words and actions align to bring clarity to their meanings.

Be transparent with everyone around you.

In my experience, I have found that a lack of clarity is usually accidental through word choice or previous experience. Withholding information or not being truthful is an intentional action that never encourages trust among team members or students and families. This should never be included in your skill set. There is no hidden agenda...ever...good or bad! However, there is a factor of confidential information that cannot be shared at times. Confidential information is not a lack of transparency, it is a variable of privacy. However, the leader should state when they need to be confidential and when they are not.

Measure what you value!

Core values, expectations, and feedback are synonymous with clarity and integrity. If your core values are aligned with your expectations and they are widely known, when you give constructive feedback, others should grow under these circumstances. However pet peeves or unclear expectations can derail your plan to increase effectiveness. Believe it or not, I have encountered principals who intentionally do not share all of their expectations with certain staff members. There is no wonder that their school cultures are toxic and they lose a tremendous amount of staff each year. I wouldn't want to work there either. Do not measure anything you have not taught as a value.

Give away more than you keep!

Great leaders are owners of responsibility and accountability. They accept and "own" any mistakes, errors, and miscues that occur. That's what leaders do! They own the problems. Your teammates need that level of support and will thrive in an environment that allows them to attempt in a fault-free zone. The flip side of that coin is that great leaders do not own praise, adulations, and prestige. Great leaders give that to their teams, staff, and organizations. In an earlier section, I referenced Jocko Willink in his book that exemplifies that spirit. "Extreme Ownership" details the responsibility that a leader has to give away the praise and own the responsibility for everyone on your team.

Be the epicenter when people need you.

Great leaders are present for their teams and organizations. Being present is not only being physically in the building. It also means listening with intention and concentration to whoever is in need of your attention. I remember when I was a teacher many years ago, there was a moment where I needed to speak with a valued leader of mine. He was standing in front of me, but I could tell his attention was nowhere in the vicinity of my conversation. I chalked it up to him having a bad day. Unfortunately, that conversation came back to bite us both. We discussed a critical need for a student in my class involving his family. That student ended up passing away in a very tragic manner. When I circled back to the leader to seek his counsel on my next steps and follow up with the family; he couldn't remember ever talking about the situation at all. He was more than a little upset. I referenced our conversation and the location to help him, but it was foggy to him. That moment, I lost a great deal of respect for him. I know it was merely his inattention that kept him from being present while he stood there in front of me. From that day on, I vowed to never be absent while speaking to someone even if I am very busy. An action I use to help is to physically move any distractions from in front of me to give my undivided attention to whoever is with me. Additionally, I clench my hands together to keep them quiet and not a distraction. In the most recent cell phone age, we see this being a distraction in many circumstances. I have let phone calls go to voicemail, text messages go unanswered, and waited to search any social media after finishing the conversation. Show integrity as a leader. They need us to!

EXAMPLE

10 years ago a young man was a soccer player at our school. He was an all state player and was featured in Sports Illustrated for his accomplishments. The previous year, we had won the state and national championships for high school soccer. Obviously, he was a special player and a wonderful young man. He became a true example of hard work, fortitude, and we all admired him. He was originally from an east African nation where the records were not kept really well. His birth certificate showed a birth date that we ascribed to for his eligibility to play high school soccer. His eligibility was never in question. However, after the season had ended, the government of his home nation found his original birth certificate. His date of birth was different than we had originally thought. He was actually a year younger than first determined. That meant he would be eligible for another year of high school soccer if we petitioned the state to re-examine his status. As a leader, I knew

that this would look nefarious and would not represent our program and school well. I decided that we should not seek to have his eligibility re-examined. Yes, we may have won another championship, but at what cost? I feel that our reputation as a school was more important than seeking another championship ring. Albeit a great opportunity, he wanted to focus on his English and graduating high school. It was tough enough coming to America at his late age and successfully finishing high school. In the end, those that disagreed with me understood after we all watched him walk across the stage at graduation. Integrity helped us all to realize that his future was better off, our school maintained its level of integrity, and I was able to uphold my convictions. I consider this a win/win.

Lead by Character

"Character matters, leadership descends for character." Rush Limbaugh

BOTTOM LINE

As a principal, you are the head of the organization. To be highly effective, you must be a suitable role model that others can respect. Your actions need to be congruent with your rhetoric. When your actions and language are congruent you are a source of stability and trust. When your language and actions are incongruent people don't know what you stand for. It is difficult for trust to develop, and they feel unsupported. The adage "say what you mean and mean what you say" is at the heart of Leading by Character.

SUCCESS INDICATORS

Determine the three words you wish your organization to be known for.

For an organization to act with character, there needs to be a clear and present focus on actions that are in alignment with the vision. That being said, select three words that you are hopeful that every student, staff member, and family will indicate represents their experience with your school. By doing this, you are establishing a hard target to align all of your actions and rhetoric to. These three words should first be known by everyone. Next, the three words should be used as a collaborative focus by everyone. Finally, the three words should be measured by the leader.

Align actions with how to treat people in and out of your organization.

Having a clear focus on the three word target lays out a visible direction to move toward. However, the processes needed to attain the targets are how you treat people in and out of your organization. Character is closely aligned with the processes of accomplishing the work of the leader. Simon Sinek (2017), renowned author and speaker, refers to this focus on process as achieving your *"How"*. The manner in which you and your organization interact with each person speaks volumes about what you believe about people and the actions you are going to take to achieve your goals. People won't remember everything their leader says. But they will remember exactly how their leader made them feel.

Make sure your actions/talk/support are congruent with the established vision.

As a final step, the leader needs to assess the impact and integrity of the processes necessary to achieving the three word goals that you have established. As with anything you value, a great leader measures the effectiveness of their goals and the fidelity to which it was achieved. I am reminded of the adage, "what you value, you measure". Once congruent, it can be replicated.

EXAMPLE

As a leader, my intentions, language, and actions must match our three word goals. I have used family-first, excellence-focused, and kid-friendly as the three goals we aspire to reach as an organization. In every exchange, my actions need to be congruent with these statements. For example, I write birthday cards for each staff member, ask about their children when a child is Ill. I tell them "go be mom". I am understanding, often to a fault, in an effort to support my family-first statement. The philosophy behind that first statement is clear. How can I as a leader expect you, an employee, to give 110% to our kids at school, if I am unwilling to let you be mom or dad in those instances where it is necessary? The culture-builder statement, "family-first" has been resoundingly a success. I hear daily how much staff enjoy being treated like professionals when emergencies arise.

Next, we established a process goal of being "excellence-focused". Being excellence-focused means that we will pursue any goal, process, or program at the level of excellence. If we cannot put the resources, time, or attention necessary to achieve a result indicating excellence, then we will not pursue it. That internal self-check toward an extremely high bar of quality, gives a clear indication to all that enter our institution that we are an organization serious about achieving our goals.

Finally, being a "kid-friendly" high school is unique in its meaning. Most high schools in America are factories of teaching. They churn out students each year that have been exposed to content. To combat this notion, we established our school to focus on GOAL (Getting Obvious About Learning) vs. GOAT (Getting Obvious About Teaching). There is a very big difference between the two statements. A school focused on teaching puts kids' needs as second to others' needs. We established that everything should be planned and developed in terms of the student. We know students' names, we talk to students, build relationships with them, and mourn when they leave us. Kid-friendly is a look at using their lens to develop our procedures and processes. This a daunting process in a school of over 3,000 kids annually.

The results are clear. We are a highly competitive and rigorous school environment that has excelled in academics, athletics, and the arts. Our kids have gone to the finest institutions of learning, played athletics at the professional level, and are working artists in a variety of fields. Staff members stay because we show that we care about them as people. Their families matter to all of us. By all of the measurables available to us, we are meeting our goals.

PART 2:
Feedback and Meta-Feedback

Great leaders aren't born. They are forged, like beautiful swords. Sword making, has, historically, been a valued and specialized skill that brought with it esteem and honor in the warrior communities. Swords have been prized for centuries as weapons of war, trophies of honor, and prized pieces passed down among the generations. These treasures have been the work of specialized artists called swordsmiths. Swordsmiths take nuggets of tamahagane iron and other materials and heat them to make a solid block of material. The material is then heated to nearly 900 degrees. It is then taken out of the fire and hammered into a long shape. The raw material is folded onto itself and the same process takes place. This process is called "shita-kitae" and is repeated from 8 to 16 times. Over and over again, heat and pressure are added to this material. Once the (soon to be) blade has been heated and folded many times, it is ground with abrasive materials to build strength. During this process the blade is heated and cooled to create stress, and then hammered again and again to harden. Finally, the polishing, decorating, and detail are added to create what we now know to be a sword. Once completed, the finished product is exquisite and beautiful, as well as deadly. This repeated forging takes time, patience, vision, skill, and constructive resistance to make a beautiful outcome.

The great leaders are formed through similar processes. Leaders are formed by difficulties or criticism, questioning one's self, gaining feedback (others and their own), and putting this reflection into practice. Just like the famous swords of the Far East, I found myself going through similar steps. Feedback and meta-feedback forged me into a leader. The development I required may not be the same that everyone needs. We are all brought to leadership by various experiences, like the raw material a sword requires to begin the forging. Whatever the material, the time and skill required varies. My beginning was unique to me. I was often described as a "dog in search of a leash".

The accolades and distinctions I have been lucky to receive are notable, but I am most proud of the organizations I have led. Finding humility, generosity, and civility as essentials to my leadership style, it's no wonder these themes keep emerging in the story of my life and my forging into a leader.

Lead Yourself

"Invest in yourself to the point that it makes someone else want to invest in you."

Tony Gaskins

BOTTOM LINE

Highly effective leaders have several leadership characteristics, many of which we cover in this series. One of the most important of these is the ability to lead themselves. A great leader must be in control of their own habits, actions, thoughts, intentions, and beliefs. To be able to adjust their performance, leaders need to gain insight into their performance instantaneously. As effective leaders, we give each other feedback on performance, but there are times when we cannot get feedback from others. In those times, we have to be able to give ourselves usable, objective feedback to adjust our own actions and achieve effective results. You cannot control what happens to you, but you can control what you do.

SUCCESS INDICATORS

Discipline yourself with things that are hard to do.

Great leaders are capable of taking feedback and using this information to adjust the trajectory of their performances to meet goals and objectives. To do so, we must not shy away from engaging in hard things. Being humble enough to adjust our actions in the face of the opinions is very difficult. However, to be successful, as a leader, this is a baseline action. No leader becomes great if they cannot do this task. To build this level of toughness, leaders should engage in other actions that require grit and tenacity. I employ several activities often to build these skills. In the past few years, I have challenged myself to do hard things by learning to play guitar, build decks in my backyard, learning to whistle, reading challenging material, learning how to podcast, and working on my motorcycle engine. All of these are skills that I do not possess. To accomplish these tasks, I had to research the elements necessary to be successful and then gain feedback from others to be successful. I intentionally trained myself to accept feedback, especially highly critical feedback.

I developed an inner dialogue to give myself feedback. I call this "meta-feedback". Meta-feedback is that voice inside your head that gives you an indication of whether your performance is effective or not. Usually, leaders are highly critical of themselves. To combat this tendency and gain usable feedback, I employ the "loved-one method". This method is simple. After a performance of any kind, pretend that you are going to give objective feedback to a loved one of yours. Simply give yourself this feedback as opposed to a loved one. This dialogue will begin the objective self talk that you need to accomplish meta-feedback effectively. Thus, making you much more highly effective in your leadership. The loved-one approach will tailor the feedback into descriptive and actionable.

Do your beliefs match your actions?

Much has been previously written here about alignment of your actions with your core values. Highly effective leaders use feedback at all times to ensure their actions are congruent with their beliefs. This proper alignment will verify that the leaders are making the necessary decisions and plans. You may feel that they are aligned, however constant feedback and the use of meta-feedback can give confirmation to the leader that they are on track.

Are your actions intentional or accidental?

There are many who will say that it doesn't really matter if a leader's actions are intentional or accidental as long as the results are present. I, wholeheartedly, disagree with that notion. Of course, results are measured by effectiveness. But, when learning effective leadership strategies and skills, replicability is key. When something happens in a haphazard way, no one can ensure that there will be replicability. I agree with being intentional in all aspects of leadership. My best thinking is that when you are consistently intentional, good things will happen as a result. You may have heard people say that you make your own luck when you work hard. Well, I believe that acting in an intentional manner will help you make your own good luck.

Do your actions stand up under the scrutiny you will receive?.

As a leader in today's world, there will be no shortage of people wanting to give their opinions of your work. There is a vast difference between people's opinions and feedback. Both are viewed, often, as scrutiny. However, there is one major distinction. Opinions are often based on emotion, often intended to be hurtful to the leader. They are made with a lack of thought. Conversely, feedback is objective. It's intended for the leader's growth, and is, more often than not, thoughtful in its construction. Of course, meta-feedback is even more reliable in its intentions. Obviously, a leader is not wanting to be hurtful to themselves, yet they can often be hypercritical of themselves. Thus, I recommend the loved-one strategy in establishing meta-feedback as a tool to improve performance.

EXAMPLE

As a leader, I make sure to rise early each day. It is my form of control over the beginning of my day. At 4:30 each morning, I get up, exercise, eat a good breakfast and arrive at school before anyone else is present. This allows me to get to school early. Once there, I check emails, sign checks, and plan my day. Then, I check my junk email. One day, this served to be critical as an email threat to the school was buried in my junk box. A very concerned citizen in a social media chat room noticed our school being targeted and reached out to me via email. Of course, our server didn't recognize this address and labeled it as junk. Consequently, checking your junk email can be beneficial. I only started checking my junk email after I received feedback from other principals that alerted me to its importance. Feedback in this manner has helped me to establish solid routines and practices that have proven to be highly effective in our work. This practice and being intentional allowed me to find this tip in my junk email box.

Lead with Intention

"Excellence is not an accident. Excellence is the result of intentional, serious effort, intelligence and a skillful execution of a vision." Gary Davison

BOTTOM LINE

Success is never an accident. Highly effective leaders are intentional. They are successful by: being prepared, accurate in their execution, and foremost in their use of feedback. The actions necessary to be intentional that lead to success are planning, diligence, tenacity, humility, open to feedback, and resilience. These are not happenstance; they are choices. Leaders choose the hard way, the work ahead of you is not always easy, but it is the right choice to make. Nike once said, "*Just Do It*". Leaders should just do it.

SUCCESS INDICATORS

Know the direction you wish to move.

Intentionality is a forthright choice into a certain direction toward the goals you have set to achieve. To move in this direction, your processes are of utmost importance. Leading with intentionality is making a firm choice once you are prepared to move. We've discussed core values and the alignment of those toward your actions. Here, we are making a clear distinction. Once a choice has been made, execute boldly and without happenstance. Commit to following in that direction and with purpose.

Know how to do the work in front of you.

To lead with intentionality, you must be aware of the processes to effectively complete the work. In addition to your capabilities, do not allow yourself to get distracted. Procrastination is an evil act of inaction that paralyzes leaders who buy into its attractions. It fills your tank to take a rest once in a while. However, the prolonged time of "rest" can become a pattern rather than a break. Make sure to stay diligent toward your process goals. Sometimes choosing to do the hard thing means simply moving forward.

Benchmark your intentions.

Establishing targets to aim at is a significant aspect of leading with intentionality. If you lead merely to achieve a result, you may miss all of the small aspects necessary to add up to a highly effective solution. That is the reason I advocate planning to complete solid processes. Intention is the motivation behind the action

Pursue (with a hunger) to hit your marks perfectly.

In the world of marksmanship, there is a wise adage: "Aim small...miss small.. Aim big...miss big" What is meant by this adage? The marksman plans for a direct hit on the target only by aiming in a focused, concentrated way toward a small aspect of the target. He is not merely happy to hit the target, he wishes to hit the exact spot on a target. This type of focus allows for precision. Precision is an intentional act by the nature of being focused and diligent toward a higher level result. There is not settling for mediocrity with intentionality. Aim small with a precise, specific goal. Nuance and sophistication of methods are actions that leaders use to aim small.

Stay the course, don't deviate, have patience and pursue it passionately.

Leading with intention implies that our focus is on the beginning of the process of leading. Nothing could be further from the truth. We, as leaders, need to be focused all the way through the planning phase, the implementation phase, and into the reflection phase of a decision or action. To keep focus all the way through the process, we need to stay highly focused and diligent toward a highly effective solution. Leaders will be excited toward the planning phase, wane a bit in the implementation phase, and then sloth-like approach the finish line of a project. I wish for a leader to maintain their energy, focus, and desire all the way through the project. An element of discipline is involved in being focused. Rather, intention means to lead your energy in a focused manner through the entire process.

EXAMPLE

When I was asked to start the high school I currently lead, it was a very intentional effort to build community from the start. My team and I set a plan for what we wanted our school to look like, feel like, and act like. There was a concerted effort on our part to model our processes after several highly effective schools around the country. We sought schools that were highly academic, some that were stellar athletic schools, and those considered to be fine arts hubs of their communities. By modeling after these stellar schools' processes, we felt assured that the results would follow. To maintain intention, we then went to our neighborhoods, churches, and temples to share the vision. Once our communities were excited, we elicited members to join us. A core of excited and intentionally focused students, staff, and community members set to work to build a stellar organization. Along the way, we set benchmarks for our processes in our annual plan. To date, we have hit every benchmark and we are known nationally in all three areas: academics, athletics, and arts. We intentionally aimed small.

Lead by Being a Teammate

"When you're part of a team, you stand up for your teammates. You protect them through good and bad, because they'd do the same for you." Yogi Berra

BOTTOM LINE

Leading a team or an organization is certainly fraught with a lot of issues, challenges, and unforeseen situations. That being said, there are many ways to lead. Most people believe that leaders must always stand in front of a group or be the first one present.

That is often the case, but not always. Great leaders can lead others in a peer to peer relationship. Not all leadership situations must be hierarchical. Even when you are the "Boss" you can lead shoulder to shoulder with members of your team or organization. Ultimately, the buck stops on your desk, but you can share the authority of your position within your organization. Shared leadership builds teammates that lead.

SUCCESS INDICATORS

Have and model an open-door policy for members of your organization.

Leading by being a teammate means that the hierarchical structure in most organizations must be leveled at times. There is still an authority component to the relationship, but access to the leader and dialogue among teammates is a crucial aspect of the open door relationship. When your teammates have unfettered access to their leader, they feel empowered to lead on their own as well. They feel closer to the seat of leadership in the organization. The freedom afforded by an open door policy rivals autonomy in terms of decision-making and access to the information necessary to make effective decisions. As leaders, we should strive to maintain that open access to all that we lead. Maintaining an open-door is easy when times are good. Adhering to it in difficult times will allow for more growth of those around you.

Show your mistakes.

There is not a leader alive today that is perfect in their planning, execution, or their effect on their organization. By showing our faults, we are allowing members of our teams to feel the autonomy to make mistakes and know that they will grow from them. As leaders, we need to provide our teammates with the feedback necessary to grow from missteps. I know that missteps occur in my leadership and I am humble enough to share them with members of my teams. Humility and growth truly go hand in hand as steps toward excellence as leaders.

Trust your charges and peers.

Great leaders develop leadership skills with their team members. Whatever manner they may use to teach skills, members of their teams need to be able to put these skills into practice. This application means that leaders should show trust and autonomy. By showing trust they are giving their growing team members the best leadership lessons that they can. Albeit important to apply, the true growth occurs when trust is given along with feedback on their performances. Leaders speak candidly, fairly, and honestly. This does not mean to be harsh, rather open and honest feedback gives aspiring and new leaders a road to follow toward their growth. Showing care will build trust.

Expect the best all the time.

Effective leaders establish the high bar of expectations for themselves. Teammates of effective leaders know that there will be high expectations and often thrive on these expectations. Many leaders will call their teams "families", however we do not really operate like we are families. I would say that we are not a family, but a loving team. Families often put up with less than stellar behavior from one another. As a highly effective team with teammates that rely on one another, we cannot tolerate subpar performance or tolerate inappropriate actions the same way we might in our family. A loving teammate would be honest with one another in their feedback on another's performance. If we keep each other accountable in regard to their performance, our organization will remain highly effective. Few families operate with this level of honesty and accountability.

Celebrate with others.

Highly effective teammates are eager to share in the victories of each other. Loving team members will hold each other accountable when positive encouragement and feedback are employed. Winning in an organization is contagious. As leaders encourage celebration of each other's wins, members encourage each other's positive performances. Teammates wish for and will help one another to earn the wins so they can celebrate with each other. One caution, however, is that honesty and truth must be factors in celebration of accomplishments. I have seen that ineffectual celebration leads to lacking or inaccurate feedback and a loss of motivation for teammates. The adage 'If everything is great, then nothing is great" truly holds value.

EXAMPLE

To treat your colleagues as true teammates in the growth of the organization, I always look for ways to connect with each member of our staff. A few years ago, I found a method that has been seen to be very successful. As I prepare each summer for the next school year, I take two days to handwrite an individual birthday card for each member of our staff. It is a time-consuming effort, but throughout the year it is highly appreciated by everyone on our team. Two hundred and forty handwritten birthday cards is a large task to undertake. However, the feeling and goodwill that teammates have on their special day makes the large effort worthwhile. My goal by doing this gesture is to establish a connection with each member of our staff by making a large staff feel small to them. I want them to know that I care and know something about each of them. After all, isn't a birthday wish a great way to show you care?

Lead by Questioning

"Good questions inform, great questions transform." Ken Coleman

BOTTOM LINE

Great leaders lead with a passion and inquisitiveness that is inspirational to those around them. They transform cultures with nudges, feedback, and suggestions in a calm and purposeful manner. Leading by questioning is often mastered early in the careers of leaders who are relatively close to their years of teaching. Great teachers use solid questioning strategies to facilitate students' understanding and performances. This skill is very much analogous to that strategy of Socratic teaching and Understanding by Design. Both of these are solid teaching practices that millions of teachers use daily to help students learn. As a leader, you use the strategies very much the same way. Rather than a curricular goal being established, the leader has a clear collaborative process established to arrive at a "best" solution. The result of this process is a collaborative culture of leadership and learning.

SUCCESS INDICATORS

Establish where you want each leader to grow.

As a leader one of your obligations is to assist the members of your team to grow in their leadership development and overall capacity. Do you fully engage your teammates in their growth? You need to set some visionary goals for their growth. This is a collaborative dance that can be done at the beginning of the school year or done in totality without the benchmarking against the school calendar. Either way, collaboratively establish goals to enhance their leadership capacity. Aspiring or new leaders will have an idea of where they need to grow, but they also need objective and constructive feedback to enhance their skill sets. Feedback is the rocket fuel to allow for growth and development of new and aspiring leaders. In my podcast, The Lodge of Leaders, I say on each episode; *"Experience is not the best teacher, feedback is..."* Use feedback as your most used tool to help those around you grow. Feedback will take you there, but know where you wish for them to grow.

Set leader development sessions to openly share feedback with your team members.

Each year, I establish Leadership Development Sessions with each and every member of my administrative team. There are currently 10 members of my team, each at varying levels of leadership capability. I plan a one-hour session to collaborate with them on their specific leadership skill sets and their goals each month. I plan these meetings to block out that time. It is a coveted time that each teammate values and anticipates. At these meetings, we discuss their leadership skill set and the trajectory of their leadership path. Objective, descriptive feedback is shared with them. We do not discuss the intricacies of their tasks. We discuss them as leaders. Solely it is a time for them to get fed and learn professionally how to plan, implement, execute, and reflect on their leadership actions. During these sessions, I use questioning techniques to elicit their responses on their planning, leadership actions, and their own reflections. The result of these leadership development sessions has been tremendous. I have seen an acceleration of their leadership growth and the dedication they have toward their own growth. I, wholeheartedly, recommend this set up for you growing your own team members.

Provide "in the moment" guidance for your team by giving guiding questions.

In addition to preset, predictable meetings with your team, great leaders provide feedback and guidance to their aspiring leaders through in the moment, real time feedback on issues. Guiding questions are the best manner in which to build decision-making strength with relevant, current topics. I have found this type of moment, along with prompting questions, builds a deep foundation of experiences and essential practice for self reflection. This provides a wonderful basis to teach leaders about the merits of meta-feedback.

Listen to the answers closely.

Great leaders are also great communicators. Communication is certainly a two-way street. Given the nature of teaching and coaching leadership, being able to listen to aspiring leaders after giving them constructive, objective feedback is crucial. Once you give them feedback in the moment of applying leadership, listening to their replies, to their application of skills, and listening to their reflections are critical to their growth. To coach team members appropriately, being able to assess their replies and guide through prompting questions gives the highest degree of likely replicability for them in their attempts. Great coaches use prompts like, "Why?", "What do you mean by…?", or "How could you have done this differently?". Go deep with the questions to drive excellence closer to attainment.

Debrief after these moments occur.

Once these meetings or opportunities to coach in the moment pass, use these chances to debrief with them. A great session of debriefing sets the tone and raises the expectation for aspiring leaders to grow in their capacities. Leaders have to learn to be highly reflective and not overly critical of themselves. Reflection is a learned skill and not one that is innate. Try the loved-ones meta-feedback method.

EXAMPLE

A few years ago, I had a member of my team that I wanted to guide and coach. He had a tremendous amount of ability. He was a bit overly eager and wanted to progress at a high rate of speed. Patience was one of the first skills I needed to be sure he embraced. Once he understood that patience is a true leadership virtue, he was able to see and use reflection in a much better manner. I had to guide him to slow down and assess things each day rather than just thrusting ahead. I was able to accomplish this through questions. Each day, I'd start each conversation with. "Why are you starting there? Tell me more about... What would you do next time?". These questions are a great disarming technique to potential leaders that are either eager, over confident, or incapable of understanding the need for reflection. Today, that eager young aspiring leader is the Deputy Superintendent in a very effective and successful school system. He has a proven track record of excellent leadership and growing other leaders. It worked well. Slow is smooth and smooth is fast. That adage was never more true than with him.

Lead by Feedback

"It is very important to have a feedback loop, where you're constantly thinking about what you've done and how it could be done better." Elon Musk

BOTTOM LINE

There are three types of feedback that coaches and leaders can use with members of their organizations. First, there is appreciation. Appreciation means to recognize someone for their effort, abilities, or performance. An example of appreciation would be to congratulate someone for completion of a task, giving someone encouraging words in the middle of a task, or even at the conclusion of a task as a reward. Next, there is coaching. Coaching refers to helping someone expand their skill set or knowledge of an area of their work. An example of coaching might be to work alongside someone attempting to give them guidance along the way. Finally, there is evaluation. Evaluation is to assess someone's performance against a set of established criteria. An example of evaluation might be the annual evaluation that an employee receives from their supervisor at the conclusion of a determined span of time. These are all types of feedback. As leaders of an organization, we will use all three of these to guide aspiring leaders, direct the organization to meet its goals, and to develop accountability in the workforce. The key is to improve performance and increase replicability.

As a leader, everything you do is directly tied to the feedback you give to others. Feedback is critical for you, others, staff, students, and community. This information allows you and others to know where to move to perform in a more effective manner. Positive feedback reinforces replication of actions, constructive feedback allows for improved performance.

SUCCESS INDICATORS

Determine the organization's core values/vision.

As with many of the skills we have discussed in these pages, determining your core values is of utmost importance in the process. Without the determination of the core values, there is no set of standards to compare anyone's efforts. Additionally, the processes necessary to grow an organization are impossible to plan with no direction in which to pursue. The lack of core values leaves an organization rudderless and without a firm direction.

Discuss the "non-negotiables" that are critical for you and your organization.

In addition to the set of core values in which to establish direction and vision, a set of "non-negotiable" expectations guide the norms of an organization. Norms and mores are also a set of expectations, however they are far less formalized. They may be less formal, but in many cases these are more understood by everyone within an organization. Albeit less formal, these non-negotiables serve as a method to contrast behavior and actions. Thus, they help us to gain feedback toward performance.

Intentionally structure consistent time for feedback.

Somewhat similar to the Leadership Development Sessions outlined in a previous section, leaders should create opportunities for feedback with all members of their organizations to improve their performance. If a leader waits for the "right time" to provide feedback, there may never be an opportunity to do so. Feedback should be consistent and not happenstance. My suggestion is to establish a culture of feedback in your organization. If it is widely known that objective, constructive feedback can and will be given at any time, the culture of improvement is embedded. A learning organization is founded on growth, not merely mediocrity.

Make constructive feedback and positive encouragement in your daily language.

Great leaders use objective, descriptive feedback as the language in which they speak to everyone in their organization. Daily language establishes what everyone knows to be the agreed-upon dialogue within an organization. True growth of an organization and its members are contingent upon a set of expectations that is followed up with performance-based language meant to improve performance. Common language and agreed-upon norms can establish leading as the standard operating procedure of an organization. This is possible if both are based on feedback being a key indicator of success.

EXAMPLE

As the principal of a large suburban high school with nearly 3,000 students, I am consistently using feedback to lead my organization. I often refer to my job as 50% setting the conditions for success and 50% giving feedback. Even when I set the conditions for success, it's based on the effects of the feedback that I have previously given. My day is often spent walking around having conversation after conversation with teachers, students, staff, and community members assessing the effects of feedback. One time, I was speaking with a teacher who was having a difficult time with a student and his parents. There was a real miscommunication between the teacher and the family regarding the student's performance. This exchange occurred in the hallway in this teacher's planning period. This teacher was frustrated as the parent was upset thinking the teacher didn't care for the student. The mother thought the teacher simply wanted to "pawn him off" to another teacher. He was being unsuccessful in her class and the parent was convinced it was because the teacher didn't care for her son. While listening, I was able to deduce that there was an overuse of educational jargon. The teacher did care deeply for the student and it was evident. She did, however, go to jargon-laced interventions that we, as educators, use to one another. I often call this " edu-speak". I shared with the teacher that she may want to call the parents and reframe the conversation without using any acronyms or jargon. The next day, I followed up with her and asked how the call went. She exclaimed that she wrote a list of things she could not say at all. She practiced and called the parents. To her delight, the call went much better and they both agreed it was a misunderstanding. The parent agreed to support her and help the student as she can. In a few weeks, the student was doing very well. At the end of the semester, the teacher received a handwritten note from the parent thanking her for taking the extra time. She now understands how to better help her son. As a leader, my discussions with members of the organization are always tied to feedback or encouragement. Nearly every discussion I have is focused around performance or setting the expectation for performance.

Lead Disciplined

"Discipline is the bridge between goals and accomplishments."
Jim Rohn

BOTTOM LINE

Many hear the word discipline and immediately think of arduous workouts, military-style determination in the face of extreme challenges, or even that annual diet that begins every January. While it may be analogous to some of those things, ordinarily nothing could be further from the truth. Discipline is simply the consistent attention of fundamental actions that lead to results. As a leader, you need to model the discipline you wish to see in others. We set routines. We need to engage in daily expectations and processes that produce effective results. This consistent focus on these fundamental skills leads to an anticipated set of routines that bring comfort and organization to otherwise chaotic situations. Why? People can trust and rely on consistency.

SUCCESS INDICATORS

Set a solid morning routine.

Each morning, I choose to set my day through several simple, yet highly effective actions. First, I choose to wake up early. At 4:30 AM, I begin my day. Waking up early has a few benefits that I cannot attain any other way. First, I am able to perform a choice of exercises that gets my blood flowing. Next, I can take my time and enjoy a good breakfast that keeps me energized and able to think properly. Additionally, I am able to get to work early and set my desk routine properly for the entire day. Of course, in my role many things happen to adjust my focus each day. However, it doesn't get me rattled as I am able to focus on my day early. Finally, I am able to welcome students, staff, and others that enter the building early in the morning. I treasure being able to smile and set a tone for each person. All of this is only possible if I can establish a disciplined, solid morning routine and be consistent in implementing it each day.

Schedule each day.

My daily calendar is a place of consistency and replication. Consistency and replication may seem boring. However, having my core values scheduled keeps me focused and moving toward success each day. Such elements that are scheduled each day in my calendar are: feedback walks with staff, opportunities to write in my journal for reflection, healthy meals, daily exercise, standing meetings that are recurring, email time, and phone calls. Having myself scheduled out in recurring fashion allows for me to have fewer changes to my schedule. This disciplined consistency helps my focus and reduces my stress level on a daily basis.

Structure meals to meet your fitness and health goals.

As leaders, we need to be healthy to be able to support and help all of those around us. A healthy approach begins with a healthy meal plan. That meal plan begins with regularly scheduled meal times. It seems to be a bit of micromanaging to establish meal times in our schedules, but I find that this routine has several benefits. They are: healthy digestion, limited thought going to meal consideration, and limited snacking throughout the day. I find it comforting to not have to worry about making meal decisions when they are already predetermined. Many great leaders have found this to be comforting.

Stay in a relaxed and calm tone.

Relaxation and calming are synonymous to effective leaders not getting distracted in the moment. Leading in a disciplined manner allows for leaders being able to stay calm and relaxed in the midst of challenging situations. A leader cannot be relaxed in a moment if it is not planned and executed consistently. We cannot merely become relaxed, we need to practice how to relax and stay calm. Doing efforts each day will prepare us for those most challenging times.

Do something physical each and every day.

A great example of leading disciplined is the leader who takes care of themselves in a physical manner. Getting a physical time planned each day can alleviate stress, increase your breathing (always good for stress relief), and calm your nerves. Such activities as walking, running, strength training, boxing, yoga, etc. can bring leaders the same results...reduced stress, clearer head, calmer attitude, and more enjoyable days. It doesn't matter what activity leaders select, as long as they do something and are consistent each day.

EXAMPLE

Every day, I wake up at 4:30 AM. I go for a brisk 3 mile walk and listen to an enjoyable podcast, digital book, or comedy radio show. It seats my mindframe mentally in a positive direction. Then, I eat the same breakfast at the same time. I enjoy my smoothie that gives me enough protein to alleviate hunger until I am ready for my scheduled lunch. In my daily schedule I have planned writing times, feedback sessions around my campus, planned workout times, and a reading block to help me stay centered. Recurring meetings are given priority in my schedule as well as my meals. All of this detail is important to me to keep my mind clear and able to attend to the needs of my organization. I am being disciplined to allow myself to be available and ready for them when they need me.

Lead by Listening

"We have but two ears and one mouth so that we may listen twice as much as we speak." Thomas Edison

BOTTOM LINE

Listening is a skill so akin to leadership that it may be difficult to separate the two. A leader doesn't manage a situation, they lead through it. Leading entails a two-way conversation that encompasses a full give and take. Highly effective leaders must be good listeners. Leading by listening means being open to honest feedback. It is imperative that we not get offended when feedback is true. Descriptive, objective feedback makes us all better. We learn to listen as a young child. Unfortunately, we soon also began talking. Leaders know that more time spent listening achieves better results. This is one of the leadership skills that we actually practice from a very early time in our lives. We are much better at this skill than we allow ourselves. Get out of your own way and listen to the other person. Don't just wait for your turn to talk. Be active in your listening.

SUCCESS INDICATORS

Go back to podcast number 52 about "Leading by Honesty" and follow the steps here.

In podcast number 52, we discussed Leading by Honesty. In that podcast, we established that the baseline of honesty is analogous to listening in a humble fashion. Humility is the action of an honest person. Thus, to be humble we need to listen closely to others. To effectively follow the advice from podcast #52, try these steps. First, know your vision so well that you can paint a vivid picture for the listener. Your vision may be clear in your own mind, but it's how well you can communicate it that matters. Next, establish crystal clear lines of communication to others from others. The clearer the lines of communication, without establishing another hierarchy, the better your ability to listen to others. Third, find the most "user friendly" time and location to be honest with others. Being honest will bring an enhanced ability to listen to others as your humility grows. Finally, great leaders model accepting critical feedback in a civil and dignified manner. Listening may be difficult, but if you concentrate on your ability to remain calm and dignified, you are likely to improve your performance.

Have a method of keeping calm when bad news happens.

Leading by listening doesn't mean that you will only hear good, happy things. Leaders are often the end of the line for complaints, grievances, or other negative comments. Once you hear the grievances, action is often required. However, to be effective we need to be able to listen fully and be completely attentive. To do so, you will need strategies to be capable of remaining calm. There are several effective practices for remaining calm. First, many leaders find it effective to use breathing techniques to stay calm. Wim Hof, world renown breathing master, trains many leaders on the pace of breathing. I find his techniques to be very effective. When in the midst of a situation, take in a large breath for a count of 5. Hold that breath for a count of 5. Finally release that breath for a count of 5. This simple technique has been tremendously effective for me in difficult situations. Next, many find that stretching or yoga are highly effective for remaining calm. Also, any physical activity can help improve calmness.

Reframe difficult questions into action language.

Great leaders take every opportunity to attempt to gain a win/win scenario. Often, it might mean taking criticism or negative comments and reframing those into action-oriented words or questions. For example, I once received the following comment on a decision I made. "Scheduling lunch like this is a waste of time and resources." After I listened completely to her comments, I reframed it accordingly back to her. My question was: "I appreciate you being so diligent about our use of time and resources, however, how can we work together to make sure this time is handled in the most effective manner possible?" I reframed her concern into a question, eliciting a response from her. My response accomplished two things. One, it let her know that I was fully listening to her concern. Two, it invited her into the decision-making process. After my response, she was now fully invested into making the decision better for everyone involved. Additionally, it gave me better information and an ally to help gain trust in the process.

Show and model not getting offended.

One of the most challenging skills a leader has to consider is modeling calmness and not being offended. Criticism and negativity are commonplace to leaders. Leaders deal with growing negativity in response to any change or a new process. When faced with criticism, leaders must keep their cool and not show signs of being offended. I have been given the most unbelievable responses in my career. Many of those responses are unfit to write here in this telling. Albeit to say, curse words, slurs, severely pointed and derogatory remarks, and insults are too common for leaders to hear in responses to their decisions. Whether the responses are in writing or are said to a leader's face, tact, calmness, and civility should be modeled by at all times. Yes, we will get upset or hurt by comments. However, if we stoop to the respondent's level by showing our displeasure, we are granting them power. I'd rather not allow my actions to give them any credibility or credence. This is a skill to practice and perfect. It is a useful ability in many applications. I have often had to smile and keep calm only to be aware that modeling this behavior advanced my vision by aligning my actions to our vision. I considered it a win for us.

Be action-oriented when listening to feedback.

As I meet and discuss feedback from others, I begin with the end in mind. Whether someone is sharing a concern or has an idea to add to a decision, I think about the end result of their opinion. If I can see the application of it in the vision of our organization, I will ask follow up questions to clarify and gain perspective. Once I have a better idea of what is being shared, I then include the speaker in the development of the action steps to apply the comment. For example, a kindergarten teacher had a concern about the use of paraprofessionals in the lunchroom, contradictory to a decision I made. It was contrary to my thoughts. We discussed her concerns and I had a chance to fully understand her comment. I really liked her thoughts. That next day, we, together, came up with a new manner of using their time to meet kids' needs. I credit her for the idea and the execution of such a daring idea. Pro tip: I gave her all of the credit and her peers loved it. She became a grade level chairperson within two years. Her respect on the team rose immediately. By being action-oriented in my listening to her, we became a better organization with a terrific idea for use of time. In addition, a respected employee gained credibility among her peers, and our culture took a step forward.

EXAMPLE

Many years ago, I was "canceled" by people who misunderstood what I meant by a post I had on Facebook. Albeit my intentions were construed incorrectly, I still realized that I offended several people and needed to do what was right to help them. As a leader, I apologized as it may have offended some people. I was hurt by that. I would never in my life want to do anything to hurt any students, teacher, or community member. I care about all of our people. However, it was more important to my team and the organization that I be humble and open to feedback. I had to listen to get better. I had to listen for our students to get better. I had to listen for our staff to get better. I also had to listen for our school organization to get better. As Jocko would say... "I was wrong? Good, I need to get better!"

Lead by Learning

"Leadership and learning are indispensable from one another."

John F. Kennedy

BOTTOM LINE

Highly effective leaders are always on the prowl to become more effective in their practice. They wish to gain experience and knowledge around their skills. Great leaders are those who are passionately seeking to improve their skills. The profile of a leader who falls into this category is clear. They are: **humble** enough to know they need to improve, they are **energetic** enough to seek improvement, they are **inquisitive** enough to ask the right questions, they are **committed** enough to actually put these skills into place, and they are **tenacious** enough to follow through with it. Leaders who do things to "get better" each and every day are more likely to develop trust with their teams, effectiveness in their decisions, and develop high-performing leaders on their teams. They become more respected in difficult times by being a learner.

SUCCESS INDICATORS

Read about leadership both in and out of your field.

Great leaders are always searching for material they can use to develop a deeper set of leadership skills. To honor the profile, they are inquisitive. These great leaders seek to find content in other fields that will help them grow. The world of sports, the military, history, and business applications all serve to enable leaders to learn skills in various settings. In this book, I have referred many times to the words of Jocko Willink. His framework has served as a guide to many principles that form my leadership skill set.

Ask questions of everyone.

Inquisitive people are showing a key indicator to great leadership. However, inquisitiveness alone is not enough to become a great leader. Once a question is posed, deep consideration and multiple points of view help the effective leader to broaden their view into a decision-making perspective. This perspective will help them gain insight into why things should happen and how to formulate the many facets to properly guide the organization.

Reflect and gain honest feedback.

Great leaders use outside readings from books and articles, they listen to podcasts and books on tape, as well as talk to leaders they respect to gain insight. Another great source of learning is one's own abilities. Great leaders seek feedback from those they respect and those in authority over them. Simply gaining feedback is not a path to greatness. Leaders need to be humble enough to elicit feedback and then committed enough to implement the feedback given to them. When receiving feedback, humble leaders ask for no sugarcoating on the feedback they are prepared to receive. Sophisticated leaders that use nuance and tact instinctually use meta-feedback. Meta-feedback is leaders giving themselves objective, descriptive feedback that guides their actions.

Do something hard!

Highly effective leaders are terribly busy leading organizations and teams to successful results. However, they are also very busy learning new things outside of the genre in which they lead. The most highly effective leaders are students at other endeavors. For many years, I learned to play the guitar as a skill to help my mind stay fertile as I was leading a large high school. This new skill acquisition allowed me to stay humble as I was taking on something that was difficult. Practicing tenacity quickly gave me a fresh way to look in the change process. Being placed in the role of student gave me a fresh perspective to look at issues in my school from a student's perspective. I am a firm believer that learning, practicing, and mastering something very difficult gives you perspective and a sense of accomplishment.

Teach someone something every day.

Leaders have the opportunity to teach people something new each day. We also are given many opportunities to share our new knowledge with others. When you are continually learning, those around you see the effect of this learning focus. They then will implement learning into their leadership development as a valued and effective strategy. Your role is to lead, but teaching is a powerful leadership tool.

EXAMPLE

During the Spring of 2020, I used the closing of schools as a chance to implement this leading by learning strategy. My mindset was either I can get better or get worse. To this end, I chose to get better. I learned a few new things. I always wanted to learn to whistle. I found videos of people demonstrating where their fingers go, how to breathe to whistle, and ultimately why I wasn't able in prior years to whistle. I learned to improve my physical health by establishing daily workouts. I had always been active before, but now I want to learn new ways and train with new equipment as a way of learning. Daily, I practiced playing guitar and working out. The results were a testament to leading by learning philosophy.

Today, I am able to give a hearty whistle when I am called upon to do so. I have also taught others to play guitar, although I am no virtuoso. My overall health improved and my stress level was at an all time low.

PART 3:
Relationships and Humility

Great leaders make great connections with everyone they meet. They seek to build relationships and act in a humble manner. These traits may be present in some people as true intrinsic characteristics. However, to be a leader, you must develop and employ these two skills. Building effective relationships to enhance leading involves a few critical skills. Among the critical skills are: emotional intelligence, growing leaders through relationship-building, developing synergy among the members of your team, following others, investing in others, and leading other generations. Additionally, the amount of humility that great leaders demonstrate is extensive. Humility goes a long way to helping develop trust, teamwork, and collaboration.

Take a moment to read about each of these skills and implement them with fidelity to become a leader who influences others through trust and uses nuance to build greater relationships.

Lead by Emotional Intelligence

"The most effective leaders are all alike in one crucial way: They all have a high degree of what has come to be known as emotional intelligence."

Daniel Goleman

BOTTOM LINE

The principalship is one of the most challenging and personally taxing professions. Long hours, emotionally draining situations, high degrees of stress, and unpredictable expectations form the average day for a school principal. To be successful in the midst of such challenges, principals need to be more than highly proficient in many skills. Some are: instructional pedagogy, leadership principles, facility management, budgetary issues, human resources management, as well as their own emotional intelligence. Leaders who cannot manage and lead themselves cannot effectively lead a team or large organization. Emotional intelligence is the keystone to principals and their leadership.

SUCCESS INDICATORS

Be attuned to positive social skills necessary to lead others.

Highly effective school leaders will need to understand and use a variety of social skills to build trust, lead various types of individuals, and develop an effective academic culture. The skills leaders need are: effective conflict resolution strategies, feedback (both positive and critical), communications methods, as well as listening strategies. I often think of my emotional intelligence skill set as a recipe that I am intending to cook. This recipe will mix to develop a wonderful and flavorful soup. However, each ingredient may be required in different measurements. Once mixed, heated, and steeped, the soup usually tastes good. This is why leaders develop a robust skill set that uses all facets of emotional intelligence. Usually, our soup is tasty.

Practice daily empathy.

Effective leaders provide all of their people ongoing and constructive feedback. One form of feedback I prefer is empathy. Cognitive empathy is the ability to take the perspective of another person and understand what their life is like. As a leader, we often need to understand others in such a manner. When we take their perspective and then give guidance we are using their feedback at its highest form. Each day, I intentionally use empathy with at least 5 people. This helps me to listen in a more clear manner. This form of emotional intelligence is critical in developing collaborative teams and employing conflict resolution.

Stay balanced in your motivation.

Great leaders will bring many valuable skills and attributes to play as they lead their organizations. These will be in various amounts across their skill sets. However wide ranging they may be, effective leaders need to maintain a level of balance. The balance that leaders demonstrate allows others in the organization to feel safety and comfort. In teams with leaders that are wildly unbalanced, members are never sure what they may encounter at any given moment. Balance breeds trust, reliability, and assurance.

Regulate your personal commitment.

Great leaders are able to stay calm in tense situations. These key skills are what keep teachers feeling comfortable and you will provide them safety and security. Being balanced with the skills you employ is critical. Of course, there will be times when we are excited, happy, disappointed, sad, etc. However, if you maintain an even keel in your demeanor, it will help those around you to enjoy the safety your skills provide.

EXAMPLE

In my 22 years as a high school and elementary principal, I have learned to stay calm. I started as a high-energy, elementary school principal that was ready and eager to change the world. It was as if I was running each and every day at a pace that was unsustainable. My ability to keep that pace wavered as time went on. It took more energy to get the team "up" because of my unsteadiness. After 5 years, I began my principalship at the high school level. The pace of high school is frantic, hectic, ever-increasing, and humbling. It was the best thing that ever could have happened to me. The frantic pace caused me to re-evaluate my effectiveness. I needed to be more steady for those around me. I needed to meet teacher needs, not my own. That revelation transformed my leadership to a deeper level. A level that sought to meet the needs of the staff and students, not just my own. This is when I learned about leading with emotional intelligence. I became balanced, attuned to the emotional needs of others, and used empathy much more. Today, I feel more equipped to lead a large organization than I could have before.

Lead by Growing Leaders

"Before you are a leader, it's all about growing yourself. Once you become a leader, it's about growing others." Jack Welch

BOTTOM LINE

The most effective leaders have dynamic skill sets and are able to do masterful things leading their organizations and teams. One attribute they share is the desire and ability to grow leaders around them. Insecure leaders don't want others to have great capacity. They wish to own the influence. Great leaders want to grow others who can, one day, take over their positions. True leadership is not about holding onto power, it is leveraging influence to benefit those you serve. Growing other leaders around you is the highest form of leadership.

SUCCESS INDICATORS

Define a process that will allow you to select potential leaders for your team.

The first step in growing great leaders among members of your team is to first select great candidates. As an organizational leader, you must determine a process that will align with the goals of your organization and the attributes of the candidates you are seeking. The process is clear and somewhat linear. Determine what you are looking for in your interviews, determine the interview process, infuse the onboarding process into your interviewing, and build excitement for the organization through your process.

I have been a high school principal for many years and have had the pleasure of growing 23 team members into executive level positions within the field of education. To do so, I had to develop an exhaustive approach for selecting team members. I started by constructing a list of what attributes I was seeking. I often sought candidates who were intelligent, hard-working, emotionally balanced, great communicators, and big thinkers. To meet these criteria, I set up a multi-staged process for interviewing. First, I read the 200+ resumes and applications of candidates that expressed an interest. Next, I boiled down the candidates to nearly 25. Then, I pre-referenced them by talking to references, looking at their past employers and asking many questions. Then, I narrowed the field down to 12. The day-of interview process has four steps: One, the candidate goes to a room with a computer and three email prompts written. I ask them to answer two as if they are an Assistant Principal here at this school. Two, they go on a tour of the building with two students. On the tour, it is the candidate's responsibility to engage and interact with the students. Later, I debrief each student. This generates a tremendous amount of information for my use in the selection process. Third, they enter a conference room with a parent playing the role of an angry parent. This scenario is used to assess their ability to problem solve, build relationships, and handle a stressful situation. Finally, they complete a writing sample used to assess their abilities to communicate and demonstrate big thinking. After all of the stages are complete, I debrief with the students, parent representative, process observers that accompany each candidate all day, and written samples. I was able to narrow the field down to 4 extremely strong candidates. This group will be interviewed individually by myself in a lengthy, scenario-based conversation. I use this format to find one candidate that I wish to grow into a building principal.

Put them into fertile ground.

Once you have selected viable candidates for growing on your team, find those great opportunities for them to grow. I like to think of fertile soil as a way to plant them, give them water and sunlight, and then plenty of tender loving care. Developing leaders is very similar. Find the great candidates and fertile opportunities for them to grow. The watering for leaders is analogous to the feedback and resources you expend on them. Resources include conferences, books, memberships to professional organizations, and any other materials you both determine are necessary for their growth. The time you spend with them is the tender loving care that they will require to grow. In good measure, your leaders will emerge as effective leaders ready to lead their own organization and teams.

Set the conditions for their growth.

As high performing leaders that are coaching others, your number one job is to set the conditions for their success. Setting those conditions include establishing appropriate expectations that are aligned with their developmental level and the goals of your organization. Be intentional about grooming them into the most effective leaders possible. That is truly only done with establishing solid expectations and standards of their behavior.

Give consistent feedback through questions not edicts.

Once you have selected great members of your team and then set the conditions for their success, you are now ready for the heat to be applied. Providing feedback to them is a continual process. I give feedback to everyone around me. The many leaders that have left my tutelage, still hear feedback from me at least weekly. Again, I prompt them through questions selected to elicit deep consideration. Feedback is straightforward, however I want them to think deeply about their performance. To this end, I will provide descriptive feedback, then use questions to have them self-assess.

Debrief everything with them.

In the growth process, aspiring leaders need to debrief all of their actions to gain perspective on their performance. They will not begin their leadership journey knowing how to assess themselves. They rely on a formal debrief until they are prepared fully to debrief themselves. This process takes at least a year. As leadership members, we are all too harsh on ourselves when we begin to analyze our own performances. However, the "loved-one" activity really helps temper this temptation. I ask the aspiring leader to give specific feedback to themselves as if they were a loved one. We always take more care when giving feedback to others than we do to ourselves. This ensures that the feedback is careful and tactful. This sets the example for ourselves to be diligent, yet tactful with ourselves.

EXAMPLE

In 2002, I was lucky enough to earn a principal position. That Spring, I was asked by the Superintendent to meet with her to discuss the next year's plans. I took several days to prepare my plans including professional learning, master schedules, instructional coaching plans, etc. I was so eager and ready to set the world on fire with my plans. The time came and we met. As I took my padfolio out of my briefcase, she got a smile on her face. It was a few minutes later when I began going through my extensive plans that she chuckled. Confused, I kept going. She finally stopped me and said the most important words ever uttered to me professionally. "Gary, I love your enthusiasm. However, I want you to focus on one critical thing. Grow leaders!" I was dumbfounded by her statement. She continued, *"If you concentrate on growing leaders, your school will be meeting every need and the staff will be able to execute any plan you wish. Grow them!"*

I took her advice to heart. In the next few weeks, I began outlining my plans to grow every staff member as a leader. In the next two years, our school went from number three academically, in our school system, to number 1 academically in the entire state. We became a model of collegiality and collaboration. This meeting and these few words set the course for the next 22 years of my career. I have since been growing leaders in every school I lead. Once leaders are growing the influence of great-thinking people will exponentially move the organization forward. She was correct!

Lead THEIR Generation

"Many recognize that simply continuing what we've done in the past will not get us to our goal. The future will not merely be an extension of the past." Tim Elmore

BOTTOM LINE

Highly effective leaders are aware of how others need to be led. Many observers often comment that we should get back to the way it used to be. Unfortunately for them, we serve others by our actions. We do not serve ourselves. As a principal for more than 2 decades, my large staff now has members from at least 4 generations. To be highly effective, I must humble myself enough to know that I serve them and need to meet their needs in association with our organizational goals. Great leaders are mindful of what others need and what is possible with the goals established.

SUCCESS INDICATORS

Know the characteristics of other generations.

I have done quite a bit of reading on the various generations within my staff and school community. To meet the needs of these various communities, I need to educate myself to their needs, motivations, desires, and common attributes. Of course, not everyone is the same, but generational knowledge will help leaders more effectively meet their needs.

The work of Dr. Tim Elmore has been influential in the awareness of generational knowledge. He has extensive writings on Baby Boomers, Generation x, Millennials, and Gen Z. They have various characteristics that vary from one another and interact in unique ways. I recommend many of Dr. Elmore's books and programs to gain insight into the interplay between the various generations.

For example, Dr. Elmore (2019) provides a basis for working with individuals from generations:

The Builder Generation (1929-1945) These folks endured the Great Depression and World War II. In general, they're frugal and know how to save money and resources. They tend to value holding on to what is right and good.

The Baby Boomers (1946-1964) These people represent the population "boom" after the war. As the largest generation to date, they felt large and in charge and expected life to be better for them than it was for their parents.

Generation X (1965-1982) This generation started with the birth control pill and Roe vs. Wade. This smaller population grew up in a broken, jaded world of Vietnam and Watergate. As realists, they know life can be hard and want to keep it real.

Millennials (1983-2000) Currently, the largest U.S. generation, they grew up in a time of helicopter parents, participation trophies, college degrees and options. They often see life as a cafeteria from which they pick and choose what they want.

Generation Z (2001-2018) This young population is still forming, but they have grown up in a time of terrorism, recession, under-employment and racial unrest. They tend to be hackers, navigating a tougher world full of social media and angst. (Elmore, 2017).

Know your team's leadership needs.

Great leaders are fully aware of what the leadership capabilities are for members of their teams and staff. No organization is fully prepared for all of its members to be effective leaders, thus leaders should know where the leadership "holes" are. Leadership holes are: which members need feedback, which need mentoring, and which need substantial coaching. You do not need to do a formal assessment, however it may be helpful to find gaps among staff members. However, listening to who leads others and watching members' actions can give you a solid idea of missing skills.

Align others' needs with strengths of your own team.

Great leaders are essentially great communicators. With a focus on effectiveness, we are always seeking to understand others. The focus on others' understanding is essential to leading their generation. Once we understand their needs and their strengths, we can align them with the goals of the organization to locate the areas of effectiveness that each can affect.

Support them in meeting others' needs.

Servant leadership is not always a notion that younger generations are often aware of. I do not wish to generalize an entire generation, but I have had the experience that proves me right. Over the years, I have had a more difficult time teaching the idea of servant leadership to young aspiring leaders. It seems to be a concept that runs counter to their values. That being said, if Generations Z is capable of being servants to others, it must be an intentional thought of theirs. Being unaware of servant leadership is a function of their immaturity. Once, we were all immature and thought that way.

Intentionally put your needs on the back burner.

Previously we discussed the notion of teaching servant leadership to younger generations as a difficult concept. It is even a farther leap to expect to see the action of servant leadership from other generations. I am not saying you won't see it being displayed, rather I imply that leaders should expect a little longer for the concept of servant leadership to be mastered. It is not a norm for their generation, so it will take longer to fully put that skill into their repertoire. They will mature. Be patient and keep leading them.

EXAMPLE

With 200+ staff members, we have a portion of our organization that is composed almost entirely by members of Generation Z. Some of which are actually alumni of our school. They are affectionately called "Double Longhorns". They are called that as a result of the school mascot benign LOnghorns, and they are two roles…former students and staff. I treasure former students who are now teachers, but I, as the leader, must treat them differently than I do the more veteran staff. We, as leaders in our organization, had to redefine how we work to support and communicate with them. Recognition, communication, and support are very different for them than for veteran staff. The younger generation is often more tender when it comes to feedback. I must be more selective of the words I choose, the locations for meetings, and the time of day for such meetings when discussing improvements or suggestions. Again, the goal is their growth. I have to consider them to grow them.

Lead by Developing Synergy

"Talent wins games, but teamwork and intelligence wins championships."

Michael Jordan

BOTTOM LINE

"Teamwork makes the dream work" was the mantra of a good friend of mine. He is now a principal of a neighboring high school. It means that simply being "stuck" together is not a unified effort. A collaborative synergy is a successful unifying effort that accomplishes objectives. Objectives and the mode of work should be agreed upon. Collective commitment is jet fuel to highly effective teams and leaders. Some organizations and leaders rely on good fortune and calmness to succeed. However, luck and happenstance are not intentional efforts. Thus, they yield very limited success and virtually no sustained learning. Synergy is the combined commitment to excellence of all the members of your team.

SUCCESS INDICATORS

Know the strengths and weaknesses of your team members.

Synergy is the combined commitment to excellence as a group. Effective leaders must first be capable of knowing the team members strengths and weaknesses to align their talents toward the organizational goals. This assessment can be done formally through a protocol or tool. However, there is sometimes variability that can throw a team askew. I often assess their strengths through my own observation and feedback. I often like to see how each member responds to the feedback I give. That facet cannot be assessed adequately in a protocol or tool. Whatever manner you choose to assess their strengths and weaknesses, having a plan to learn them and align them is key to the success of your team.

Know how to communicate effectively with each member.

Team synergy is heavily reliant on the ability of the leader to communicate effectively with the team. To be the leader that leads with synergy, there must be trust and commitment toward the leader. These key facets take time and intention to achieve as the leader. Many leaders skip the trust-building phase and go straight to the commitment phase. Please do not short change the need for building trust. Trust is the glue that keeps relationships together. When relationships are on solid footing, feedback and commitment can be driving forces into the learning and success of the team.

Communicating both with the team and with individual members are contingent on the trust established. However, team communications are also dependent on the commitment to one another. There is a renewed effort of many to use team-building and activities to establish a bond between team members. Know your team and what activities or protocols will be most effective with them. I remember a colleague once took his team to the gun range as an activity to bond them together. However, two members of his team were vehemently against guns of any kind. Unfortunately, this choice became a point of division rather than a bonding activity. There are several factors to consider when attempting to lead with synergy.

Plan for success indicators for your team.

Synergy among team members is a process to succeed as a team. However, this process can be planned to eliminate errors and mistakes. As the leader, you can make plans to bond members together emotionally, intellectually, and physically. However, highly effective leaders plan for benchmarks along the easy path to success. Set interim goals leading with synergy. Norms for highly effective behavior can be success indicators for the ability of your team to lead with synergy.

Give constant feedback to each member.

Trust and belonging to the team are major factors leading to synergy. To establish a deep level of trust and commitment, feedback is a critical feature. Not only do leaders need to provide feedback on team member's performance, but feedback on their level of commitment to the goal is vital. As trust is established more detailed and objective feedback can be shared. Start slow and build a culture of productive, helpful, objective feedback to establish a trusting culture among your team.

EXAMPLE

In my administrative team, I currently have 10 members. There are varying levels of experience ranging from 0 to 13 years of leadership experience. Each of them have different levels of experience and abilities in varying areas. This past year, I added two new members to our team. When I composed the executive team for my organization, I sought to build the team based upon collective strengths and weaknesses. Experience, energy, intelligence, high commitment, and support are major factors for my team to be able to act synergistically. Once the team was assembled, I intentionally planned to establish opportunities to develop synergy through activities, time spent together, common goals, and established norms. We started by attending a retreat together for three days. This activity has had varying results in the past, but this current team responded very well. They started to bond and develop trust almost immediately. Each day that has progressed has been another step toward a full example of leading with synergy. Since the summer retreat, they have become a finely tuned team that enjoys, respects, and brings out the best in each other. Our administrative teams has never operated at such a high level. I am so thrilled.

Lead by Following

"A leader is best when people barely know he exists, when his work is done, his aim fulfilled, they will say: we did it ourselves.
—Lao Tzu

BOTTOM LINE

Principals may be the leader of a school, but principals often follow as well. We follow policy, practice, good sense, we delegate and give feedback as a follower would. We also follow trends, feedback from staff, students, and the community at large. As a leader, the main point of following is to put yourself in the shoes of another person. Following is analogous to empathy from that perspective. A leader should stand in the shoes of the people we are leading. This perspective change will give leaders the necessary vantage point to understand the nuances and sides of any given point. Leading by following means to lead with a perspective that sees all aspects of any situation.

SUCCESS INDICATORS

Understand the parameters in your organization.

There are systems we have to follow at all times. There are board policies, system practices and procedures, as well as building and organizational norms. Great leaders understand them and the need for them. Additionally, great leaders see these "immoveable" parameters as borders or boundaries to act within. They are guardrails for them to use their creativity and knowledge to lead within. However, there is one more area that great leaders follow. That is in terms of seeing perspective from the viewpoint of those who follow their leadership. Being empathetic and understanding is a form of leading by following. When acting from the perspective of those you lead, being a follower is a great tactic for effective leadership.

What are the norms of your community?

Highly effective leaders know that following the norms of your community and organization are critical to be successful. Norms often shift and change. Staying abreast of changes is a great way to lead by following. We already discussed following policies and procedures, but norms are more critical to the culture and climate of the people in an organization than merely policies.

Does this decision make good sense?

Highly effective school leaders make many decisions in an average day. Great leaders who lead by following will make certain they are evaluating their decisions through a very simple lens. That lens begins by the leader asking if the decision makes good sense. This seems very elementary in its make up, but this lens can keep aspiring leaders focused as complicated variables arise that are not pertinent.

What are the growing trends in your school community?

Leading by following seems counterintuitive in a book about growing your leadership. However, evaluating information and data can grant the leader perspective that can change the dynamic of a decision. For example, dynamics in each school community that change over time. Some variables that change can be demographics, programs, personnel, and budget. Understanding the changing dynamics and being up to date on those can make leaders into highly effective leaders very quickly.

Be a servant leader.

Great leaders rely on servant leadership as a basis for their influence and relationship? When acting as a servant leader, you are actually following the needs of others and not simply stating what others need. This is a small distinction, but a crucial one. You are following the need, not the person. Much is written about the leader being in front and being the most active in discussions. However, servant leadership throws that notion on its ear. Following the needs of someone rather than being the person that others follow is a roundabout to deeper leadership. People want and desire to have their needs met. If you, as the lea0der, can meet those needs, you will have a follower of your leadership.

EXAMPLE

I am currently principal of a large suburban high school. We opened this school in 2009. Our school has been, and continues to be, an academically focused high school. Our graduation rate exceeds 99% and over 98% of those attend post-secondary education after high school. Over the last ten years, I have been following the recent trends among students and their desires for coursework. From 2009 to 2012, over 50% of our seniors completed their graduation requirements and exceeded them by taking 6 years of World Language courses. That trend reflected the desires of our state universities and elite colleges. However, since 2013, I have witnessed a shift among the desires of our students. Over 50% of students are now graduating with in excess of 6 years of science courses. This shift began as a gradual slide from world language courses to science courses. However it has accelerated recently with the pandemic. Additionally, we opened a healthcare science program in 2014. As a leader, I need to follow this trend and understand the reason for the change. If I led as a reactionary leader would, coursework would not be ready, teachers would not be prepared, and budgetary constraints would overwhelm our shift. Rather, we lead by following with an established budget and facility priorities, as well as certification and staffing additions to match the change. Highly effective leaders will follow the trends and needs of students and staff to prepare their organizations for the shifts that inevitably result.

Lead by Investing in Others

"Invest your time with people who will push you to be your best. Winners love to see other people win." Chalene Johnson

BOTTOM LINE

Great leaders grow themselves and grow their organizations. Great leaders, on the other hand, grow others first before themselves. This nuanced approach actually brings greater depth to their organizations. This approach leads to robust cultures. Successful cultures are a result of an intentional action for growing everyone around them. When an organization has a culture of *"We are a team...We will learn together...and We will win together"*; they define excellence by giving to others in their organization.

SUCCESS INDICATORS

Know your team.

One of the hallmarks of great leadership is knowing your people very well. Great leaders have intentionally gotten to know the members of their teams. They know their strengths and they know their weaknesses. This depth of ability knowledge gives the leader a wonderful place to align opportunities to members. However, some leaders choose to just take what they're given and not invest in the team. They lead by hoping. They hope that the members of their teams will, somehow, gain the ability to lead. This lack of intentionality is what I call, leadership negligence. Leadership negligence is the lack of intentionality of investing in others. They simply settle for hiring for ability. This fallacy falls short. Members have a ceiling that they can never break though

119

without your guidance, feedback, and intentional effort. Deeply knowing the abilities of your team is the best way to start to invest in others.

Set the Conditions for Success.

Simply plopping a person down in the middle of a situation isn't actually investing in them. To properly invest in others, a leader must be aware of setting the proper conditions for their success. That begins with knowing their abilities, knowing situations that can bring them experience and then providing them with objective and descriptive feedback. To further set the conditions properly a leader needs to: provide resources necessary, allot time for feedback (from the leader), as well as, reflection (meta-feedback), and finally allow them to apply their new learnings in a risk-free environment, suitable for growth.

Develop their individual goals together for their growth.

Intentionally planning goals and directions together are universal in the world of learning. Albeit, we are learning to lead. For this transaction to occur, the leader must help set goals with each individual they wish to grow. These individual leadership goals are collaborative in construction and visionary in their reach. Anything short of this level of intentionality is merely wishing for growth. A gardener will plant a flower and then give it light, water, and attention. Even flowers don't grow without the proper attention to their needs. Aspiring leaders need no less attention and deserve much more.

Align all growth with the vision of the organization.

As the head of an organization, leaders have their eyes constantly to the vision. Great leaders balance this attention with the abilities and growth needs of members of their teams. This alignment allows for members' abilities to grow while moving the organization toward their vision. By looking for opportunities to have overlap, the needs of the organization and aspiring leaders can be met at the same time. Congruence should be a close alignment. One should never try to change the needs of the organization to fit the needs of an aspiring leader. Opportunities will arise in good times. Leaders should be patient, knowing that there will be potential opportunities.

It is the obligation of the leader to find these opportunities. It's not their obligation. They are to be focused on growing, you, as the leader, are to be focused on alignment.

Give constant feedback to everyone.

As with any learning endeavor, there is one true pathway to learning leadership. Aspiring leaders are taught suitable processes and skills to implement. Once learned, these skills need to be attempted in a real-world context. Once the skill is attempted, constructive, objective, and descriptive feedback needs to be given. This step cannot be short-changed, nor ignored. I find this to be the most fundamental aspect of learning any leadership skill. Intelligent people can read about any skill, however, implementation and feedback are key to mastery. As leaders, we are seeking high-level mastery and not merely attainment. This feedback is critical to skill development as the learner needs to be able to make adjustments based upon their progress. Objective measures toward their progress are very difficult to attain without the assistance of a mentor or leader providing guidance.

EXAMPLE

A few years ago, there were two new members on my executive team. They had different needs from one another as their skills and abilities were different. We'll call them Hillary and Micah. Hillary and Micah were extremely talented and were full of potential. I selected both of these leaders through very arduous selection processes. They were what I consider to be "top shelf" potential leaders. Their potential aside, they both still had substantial work to do to be considered ready to lead their own organizations. In comparison, Micah and Hillary were very different. Micah was gregarious and outgoing with a salesman's approach to meeting and collaborating with others. He was a former social studies teacher and was very knowledgeable. His potential for the soft skills was extremely high. He knew the ability to get a conversation going with someone else. Hillary, by contrast, was more of an introvert. Seemingly very quiet, she was not shy at all. She was more quiet until engaged in a conversation. Then, she came alive when discussing with teachers. Hillary was also a former social studies teacher and very knowledgeable. Both were excellent teachers in the classrooms. Their collective instructional acumen was very high.

They were both at the same organization at the same time. So, we can compare the intentionality for investing in each as their needs and abilities were different. Aligning their needs with the organization was my responsibility and could not look the same. I need to make this abundantly clear for them as they understood what my intentions were. With them both on board, we began.

Micah was a highly engaged visionary leader. He could see the outcomes of processes and their effects on others. Thus, I worked with him to fine tune these abilities and become more effective at concrete processes. This was not his strength, however. He also was a more hierarchical thinker. This meant that he was very concerned about the chain of command. I, too, respect authority. However, to be his best visionary leader, I needed him to be able to translate his thoughts into words that others could understand. It was a tough task, but he embraced it fully.

Hillary was an extremely thorough, detail-oriented worker. She was always the first to begin and the last to finish. She was highly concerned that every detail of anything she attempted was perfect. Her abilities were remarkable. She, too, was a very hierarchical thinker and I was worried that it might impede her. However, her ability to translate her thoughts was a strength of hers. We worked to fine tune that strength and develop more visionary practices. She took to the development of vision like a duck to water.

Both of these outstanding aspiring leaders had grown substantially. They were both extremely successful high school principals. After their tenure as school leaders, they both became district leaders. I am very proud of the work they both did to accomplish this level of growth.

Lead through Relationships

"The most important single ingredient in the formula of success is knowing how to get along with people." Theodore Roosevelt

BOTTOM LINE

Leading through relationships is a very simple concept. However, there are many aspiring leaders who get mired in the minutia. There are three basic reasons that great leaders lead through relationships. First, building solid relationships as a leader enables that leader to build trust among everyone in their organization. Trust is the essential element in leading any group of people. Trust is especially important as many of the decisions you make can involve members having to accept and understand the need to change. To bring others along in the change process, members must have a level of trust in their leader. Second, to ask a member to apply any duration toward a difficult task, members need to rely on the trust they have in their leader. Finally, trust establishes a collaborative environment where members can feel safe enough to be able to give and receive feedback as well as instruction toward challenging goals. Successful leaders are those who build caring cultures. People will follow a leader, long term, who cares for them.

SUCCESS INDICATORS

Know the names of all your staff members.

As we approach summer each year, I give a newly printed yearbook to my executive staff. Over the summer, I ask them to review the pictures and learn the names of staff members in our organization. Our organization has more than 200 staff members. Our campus is also extremely large and very spacious. There are many in the organization who may never see one another. Add to that fact, there are upwards of 20 new staff members each year. To effectively build relationships with staff members, the first step is to know their names and then begin conversations with them. Knowing their names is the first step to building the trust necessary to being a collaborative organization. To continue to build relationships with staff members, I recommend keeping a file for each staff member and adding pertinent details about them. Such information could be: childrens' names, spouse's name, background employment, any interesting things about them, etc. After you've known them a while and have become familiar with their information, you will not need the file system any longer. However, make a file for each new staff member until you fully know them.

Be involved with your staff.

When I think of leading through relationships, I am reminded of the movie, "The Wizard of Oz". Remember how Dorothy and the rest of the ragtag group wanted to meet the Wizard? All they wanted to do was to meet and explain their situation. They knew in their collective hearts, even though the tin man didn't have one, that he was able to help them. When I meet principals that stay in their offices more than they are in the building, I think of the scene that made Dorothy really disheartened. When Toto tugged on the curtain to reveal that the Wizard was a simple man with a camera and sound effect machine, their collective world fell apart. Up to that very minute, they revered the Wizard and held him in high esteem. Once the truth was revealed, all of their hope was lost. More importantly, trust was lost.

Leaders often find themselves in similar situations. Great leaders are not hiding behind their office door or stuck behind a desk at all times. They must be involved with staff to build a trusting relationship. This involvement can look very different by location, level, and size of organization. Stepping into classrooms, sitting in on planning meetings, stopping staff in the hallway, talking about them as people, discussing students' situations, and supporting them at difficult times are all examples of being involved with staff. Trust is the effect of all of these actions. Face to face interaction is key to building effective trust.

Know your students' names.

In the same effort as getting to know staff members' names, I ask my executive team to study the yearbook I give each of them. As a leader of a learning organization, it is vital that we learn not only the students' names, but know about their families. For example, as a high school principal, there are 3,000 students in our school. I have been at this school for several years and have now had the siblings of many students currently in our school. This generational knowledge is very important for my leadership. This knowledge is so critical that I ask for a list of the recurring names of students we have had to better understand building relationships with families and the community. Again, trust is critical for leading through relationships. What better way to build trust than to be a significant positive force in a family's experience?

Go to as many student events as you can.

As a principal, parents, students, and the community expect to see the leader at student events. Relationships are built and reinforced through collective support at academic, athletic, or arts events involving students. Students take a great amount of pride in preparing themselves to perform well, and we can reinforce a great relationship by complimenting their efforts and their successes. Not only is it a great deal of fun to attend these events, a tremendous amount of effective work toward your ability to lead through relationships is built during these off school hours. It really matters to everyone in the organization.

EXAMPLE

I have learned many ideas over the years about building relationships with members of our teams. One that is particularly positive revolves around each staff member's birthday. Each summer, I take 2 days and write a handwritten birthday card for each staff member. It takes a lot of preparation and is quite arduous to write 240+ birthday cards. However, the goodwill this gesture establishes is tremendous. As the years have progressed, I have been told many times how much this simple gesture means to our team. I have even come to enjoy doing this task and watching the smiles on each of their faces as they read their cards.

PART 4:
Vision and Direction

As I think about vision and direction, I am often reminded of the quote by the legendary hockey great, Wayne Gretzky. He was asked by a reporter how he was always in the right place every time the puck came by. Gretzky said, "I skate to where the puck is going to be, not where it has been." The Great One, as he is referred to, meant to be successful, highly effective leaders must aim toward a destination that will allow them to be successful. Skating to where the puck has already been is akin to leaders following outdated methods or procedures that are not aligned with success indicators for your organization's goals. Having a firm idea of what success looks like is a trait that vision and direction will help to accomplish. Leaders must not only have a vision of where the organization will go, but also the direction to know how to get to the destination. These are two sides of the same coin. That coin is an organizational movement toward success.

Lead toward Vision

"Good leaders create a vision, articulate the vision, passionately own the vision, and relentlessly drive it to completion." Jack Welch

BOTTOM LINE

As a leader of a learning organization, I have always established a vision that is based on the processes necessary for success. Great leaders have always believed that if solid processes are written, pursued relentlessly, and achieved with fidelity, the results will follow. Be obsessive when pursuing the processes of excellence. Vision is a crucial first step for a leader's plan for any organization. By setting a direction, it is clear that all members need to be aligned. This unity of purpose brings congruence to all facets of the organization. This unity increases clarity of purpose, the likelihood of success, and focused efforts for all members of the organization.

SUCCESS INDICATORS

Establish a process-laden vision of what excellence looks like for your organization.

Leaders, great and mediocre, all want their organizations to achieve success. However, one factor that separates great leaders from the mediocre leaders is being able to identify and communicate what success looks like to their organization. The vision necessary to achieve greatness should be composed of processes and not results. If results are the vision, isn't it simply a wish? Vision will communicate to everyone where they are going. The results are simply a destination. However, a complete vision will give the end destination as well as the benchmarks, along the way. For example, I have been principal of the same high school for several years. When we opened the school in 2009, we began with a vision that was very process heavy and also dialed in the results we wanted to achieve. It was: *"At Lambert High School we will align our processes, culture, and resources for ALL of our students to compete at the highest level."* Note that this vision statement is clear in what the organization will do and what it is seeking to accomplish.

Communicate this vision to every member of your organization.

Good leaders establish a solid vision and pursue it with vigor and exacting accuracy. However, great leaders will establish a solid vision, pursue it diligently, model it continually and will communicate the vision with each and every member of their organization. This communication allows for a deep understanding of the vision among all members of the organization. It's this step toward involving each member of the organization into the work that separates good leaders from great leaders.

Live the vision with all of your actions.

All eyes are on the principal of a school at all times. Whether we like it or not, principals are held up to a certain standard. Oftentimes that standard may be unattainable. However, great leaders are not only cognizant of this but appeal to this to guide their actions. The blueprint they use to set their path is the vision of the organization. If we have a guide to our daily actions that are congruent with the direction of the organization and aligned with our own personal vision, then we are modeling the most appropriate actions for our team members and students to see. This not only allows the leader to bring the vision to life, but guides visible actions to show the way for all to follow.

Give feedback to others relative to the baseline of your vision.

There is no secret that feedback and vision are critical to the success of any leader and organization. Using every moment as an opportunity to share feedback with others allows the leader to establish a baseline of expectations and a language to frame their leadership discussions. It has often been said that feedback is the language of leadership. There have never been truer words shared about the development of leaders. Use feedback as a framework for your language with team members and there is a strong likelihood their performance will increase. Focus on both types of feedback, positive (encouragement) and constructive (improvement). Use both in equal measures and when most appropriate for the situation.

Do the same for your own feedback.

The emphasis on leaders providing feedback to team members is critical. However, who provides feedback for the leader? In most learning organizations and schools there is only one leader. That leader is often the principal. If we are led by feedback and there is only one of them in a building, who guides them? This scenario is a perfect framework for principals to use meta-feedback to guide themselves. Principals can develop the internal dialogue necessary to gain feedback from themselves. It is a process to be able to learn this skill. Simply listening to one's intuition is a great start. However, over time, great leaders are able to refine and delineate what is a fear notion and how to guide their own feedback. One step I often guide aspiring leaders to use is the "loved ones" method. The Loved Ones method is to stop your inner dialogue for a few minutes and give yourself the same objective, descriptive feedback you would give to a loved one who acted in the same fashion. What would you share with your son? Father? Mother? Sister? etc... After you determine what that feedback would be, simply take a moment and give it to yourself. Next, ask yourself how fair this feedback was. At the conclusion, you will have set an inner dialogue baseline to hold up as a standard for your effectiveness.

EXAMPLE

In 2008, we were preparing to open a new high school in the school system I have been working for years. I was asked to be principal of this high school. It was such an honor and I will forever treasure the experience. To begin the work, a few trusted team members and I worked together to establish a vision of what we hoped to achieve. We had found several schools around the country that had components we liked. They each achieved results in areas that we wanted to be successful. Those areas were: academics, athletics, arts, community involvement, and student support. We then looked at the purposes and processes they used to achieve their individual results. However, we wanted to achieve them all. Not simply one specific area. That would serve to be a challenge.

When we started the vision of the organization upon student support. in each area support would be the critical process to focus. Our belief was that with enough support, our students could achieve greatness in each and every area of focus. Our team came up with our vision in terms of process and achievement. *"At Lambert High School we will align our processes, culture, and resources for ALL of our students to compete at the highest level."* So our path was written. Now we simply had to pursue it.

15 years after setting this path, we have had many achievements and accomplishments. Our organization, Lambert High School, has accomplished tremendous achievements in academics (platinum level recognition from the state), athletics (dozens of state and national championships), and arts (multiple national and international championships and awards). By infusing community involvement and student support as core elements of our work, each area benefited greatly for student success. I would credit much of the success to casting a vision that not only allowed for results, but cast in stone the processes necessary to achieve these results.

Lead by Example

"The most powerful leadership tool you have is your personal example." John Wooden

BOTTOM LINE

Great leaders use their influence to encourage their team members to improve their performance. Ultimately, leadership is all about influence. If we, as leaders, can positively affect the outcome of a member's performance, then we have achieved our objective.

There are several ways we have discussed to accomplish this action. One is by the words we use. People get excited by words that leaders speak, but their respect for you grows by watching your actions. You must walk the walk after "talking the talk". Another is through our actions. Leaders' actions can be the positive example that members need to follow for their performances to improve. To lead by example, I often recommend that leaders under-promise and over-deliver.

SUCCESS INDICATORS

Be highly visible.

Great leaders are highly visible to all members of their organization. There are times where leaders cannot be present in large groups. However, it allows for leading by example to be front of mind when we are present with our teams. Visibility is an action of attention and a framework that allows for relationship-building and feedback opportunities. Great leaders don't hide from others...they embrace the times to be seen. Being seen is a trust-building action.

Narrate your actions to your team.

Team members and aspiring leaders search for direction even when direction has been provided by a vision. They are not looking for contradictions, rather they are looking for confirmation that their actions and beliefs are congruent with their leader. For this reason, great leaders should accompany their actions with a dialogue that helps to translate the purpose of their actions. This congruence lends credibility to both the leader and the stated goals being displayed. Confirmation always trumps cloudy when being visible with team members. They often need a soundtrack to accompany their modeled actions.

Be intentional.

Great leaders often deal with unforeseen situations and crises. However, their plans, goals, processes, actions, and results are highly thought out. Ongoing, successful results are never accidental. For continued excellence, planning and intentional actions are key. Be the leader who is intentional in all things. Autonomy is not the antithesis to intentionality. You can intentionally plan and give autonomy on how to implement a plan. They are not diametrically opposed to one another.

Debrief your planning and actions with your team.

Just like great leaders narrate their actions in the moment, these same leaders will debrief after a situation has come to resolution. Take a moment to sit with your team or those you intend to grow and display your thinking from the planning to the execution of a project or plan. This will demonstrate for your team that intention was allotted and this is not an accidental success. We cannot always hire the rock stars that we hope for. Often we need to train up those around us to become top performers. The best way to do so is to provide the ongoing dialogue they need to understand how great leaders operate. Remember, great language plus great feedback equals great leader development.

Demonstrate ownership.

Great leaders are not perfect. When they act with intention and use proper planning, sometimes things still go awry. Have no fear that you must be perfect in all circumstances. You simply do not. Even the best leaders make mistakes. However, the great leaders embrace the mistakes and even display ownership of those mistakes and unforeseen circumstances. The truly elite leaders also take ownership of mistakes that affect the organization that others make. Jocko Willink (2015) in his book "Extreme Ownership" presents this idea in detail.Many leaders have embraced this philosophy. It has been my experience that when using Extreme

133

Ownership the trust among team members has risen to unforeseen heights and the collaboration increased substantially as well. Thus, leaders grow by owning their circumstance.

EXAMPLE

As a young, first-time principal, I sought to use leading by example in as many ways as I could. I intended to build a collaborative and supportive environment for the new staff that I was serving. It was a large, suburban elementary school with a staff of 73 team members. One area that I found that I could lead by example was during bus duty. Our school was positioned at the top of a hill and the road had a severe turn prior to the entrance to our parking lot. Each afternoon, buses would line up at the entrance and it was perilous for them to enter the road. To both help the buses and students be safe in the afternoon as well as lead by example, I took this opportunity. Each afternoon, I would hold the buses until all of the students were loaded. At that time, I would grab a portable stop sign and ride the first bus to leave the campus. At that time, I would exit the bus and enter the road. Once there was a safe clearing, I would stand in the middle of the road and hold all of the oncoming traffic. This allowed each and every bus to enter the road safely. After several weeks, the parents driving in traffic understood what I was attempting to accomplish. They even helped with their speed and slowed as they approached the entrance. It was scary a few times, however by setting the example to my staff, students, and the community I feel we were safe. Additionally, the respect garnered by my example went a long way to setting a tone of service and humility. This aided our move toward a highly collaborative environment.

Lead by Deciding/OODA Loop

"Highly effective leaders know when and how to make thorough, quick decisions and then live by the consequences in the moment."
Gary Davison

BOTTOM LINE

At times leaders must be able to act effectively and quickly. There are many decision-making protocols that exist in the leadership and business worlds. However, there is one that I have used many times and have found tremendous success with. The OODA loop is a decision-making protocol that you can use in the moment of a crisis. It is a time-sensitive approach to handling a decision. Developed by John Boyd, United States Air Force, in 1976. It is a method for combat pilots to make quick, effective decisions. Obviously, in the setting of a jet pilot, time is of the essence. As a leader, having a decision-making protocol that is time sensitive is important to have at my discretion. There are instances where time is a critical factor.

SUCCESS INDICATORS

The four steps of the **OODA Loop-**

Observe- In the *observe* phase a leader will take in all the necessary information that can affect the positive outcome of a situation. This is where a leader will discover unfolding circumstances and collect all the information regarding those circumstances.

Orient- During the *orient* phase, a leader will analyze and synthesize the information they have gathered. At this point they will use past experiences, culture and traditions, as well as any new information that arises. This is the phase where the alignment of the situation and information come together.

135

Decide- In the *decide* phase a leader begins the decision-making process. Here they will make a hypothesis based upon the information and the alignment of that information. In this phase a leader will say "We will act…"

Act- Finally, in the *act* phase a leader will implement the action selected in the decide phase. It is a move into action and a test of your hypothesis…

The OODA Loop is a fast-paced decision-making process that allows for changing variables, instantaneous changes in direction, and repetition of the process again and again. In a given crisis, I have gone through the OODA Loop as many as nine times prior to finding an eventual solution.

EXAMPLE

It was a clear spring morning arrival. Nearly two-thirds of our 2,500 students were on campus and the bus lanes, car rider lane, and student parking lots were full. As with any large high school, there was a constant buzz of energy taking place as kids were hustling from one place to another. As I was standing in the hallway greeting students, I heard a staff member running down the hall towards me. He indicated that Linda, a trusted and loved library aide, was on the floor. I ran toward where she was lying. She was face down in a pool of her own blood. Apparently she had fallen and hit her face on the wall and her head on the floor. I was not sure of any other injuries at the time. Unfortunately, as I rolled her over I noticed that she was non-responsive and not breathing. In this tumult of emotions, I relied on the OODA Loop to help me plan our school response. I began to accumulate the information I was able to observe. Next, I oriented the information with a few other facts. One, she was not breathing. Two, she had previous health concerns. Three, getting an ambulance would be difficult as the roads were all jammed around the school. At that moment, I called our School

Resource Officer and he jumped the curb with his car and drove along the grass to get close to the building. At this moment, our nurse was performing CPR and using the AED (Automatic External Defibrillator) on her. Her heart stopped. That new information caused me to go back to step one in the OODA Loop. I gained new information and began to orient this new information. Instead of planning on a situation where they would work on her here, I planned on an immediate evacuation of her. Time was of the essence.

In the next few minutes, the SRO cleared a path for our ambulance to cross the fields to the door. I coordinated staff members to escort kids to other doors. We "deputized" kids to be hallway monitors on closed hallways for us. Our response began to work like clockwork. The EMTs that attended for us were magnificent. They began to work on her. She was quickly swept away on an ambulance gurney and taken to the hospital. The EMTs had indicated that she was unresponsive and had no heartbeat at all. She was out on the floor in our school.

At that moment, I along with our Athletic Director jumped in his car and sped to the hospital. We were not allowed into her room to see her, but the indication was that she was in very bad shape. Fortunately, the story has a very good ending. She was brought back to life. She returned to work several months later. She had a full blown heart attack which then caused her to fall face forward into the brick wall. Her face and head injuries were the cause of the pool of blood. She had lost several teeth also in the fall.

The use of the OODA Loop caused us to realign our emergency protocols to be able to adjust as new information becomes available in the midst of any situation. Had we not been able to act quickly, change our direction, and follow up effectively, I am afraid of what the outcome might have been.

"Lead by Deciding/Acting (WILL)"

"Highly effective leaders know when and how to make thorough, quick decisions and then live by the consequences in the moment."
Gary Davison

BOTTOM LINE

At times leaders must be able to act with deliberate and willful action. Yet, they still need to seek to be highly effective. WILL is a decision-making protocol that you can use when you have more time to be able to plan. In this protocol, time is not of the essence as it is in the OODA Loop. It is an information-rich approach to handling a decision. It is a midpoint between the OODA loop (very quick) and the Constant Analysis (methodical) approaches to making decisions. Likely, this protocol will end up being a "go to" as it can be used more often in "typical" types of decisions. It is intended to be a "one or two and done" type of protocol. The OODA Loop, however, is intended to be used over and over and over again with speed and precision.

SUCCESS INDICATORS

> **WATCH**- In this stage, leaders will do similar actions to the OODA Loop by collecting information, and observing to gain as much information as possible. This can be a long-term approach as it is not time sensitive.

> **INFORM**- Here the leader is analyzing information. They have the time to see patterns emerge that can inform their planning. They build steps and execute detailed planning to set the best course possible. Again, time is not as much of a variable and time can be allotted. Yet, inaction is very destructive in this stage.

LEAD- Leaders will intentionally act with the plan. Since time is a low level variable, the team can look around for changing variables and new details. Leaders are encouraged to be flexible and pivot as necessary. Here, the rubber meets the road in the execution of the plan.

LEARN- A thorough debrief is key to the organization and team members executing in the future. In this stage, leaders analyze results and patterns. Team members are also asked to elicit feedback from members of the team. A solid debrief and reflective opportunity will help everyone grow and the organization to get better each time the process is taken.

EXAMPLE

I have used the WILL protocol for many years to teach my team about how to make a decision. Analyzing this information for its impact on many variables is often challenging for new leaders. This is a perfect system to use for their learning. Gathering new information is a comfortable skill for new leaders. However, they often get stuck in the analysis phase. This method is highly dependent upon being humble enough when feedback points to improvement.

Each time I meet with our administrative team, I find this protocol to be very helpful as we work through new planning for decisions. Recently, we planned a new event for our rising freshman to become introduced to our school. We met as a team and started our planning. In phase one we gathered as much information about what it was we hoped to achieve with this event. Our team gathered information about the students and the elements we wanted them to get from attending. Phase two took several days as we researched what other schools had done in a very similar vein. Patterns began to emerge and we used those patterns as information to aid our planning. On the day of the event, we began phase three. We acted. The event went well and the kids had a terrific time. They provided us with feedback and the staff members gave their feedback as well. At the next administrative meeting, we reflected in phase four and looked for ways to make the event better for the future.

Again, this process is not time sensitive, but time is a small factor. At the end of the day, the process worked very well for our planning and allowed for many team members to collaborate and work together. The learning that each was able to articulate proved that the protocol worked well and the learning was effective.

Lead by Core Values

"Your core values are the lifeblood of your leadership instincts."
Gary Davison

BOTTOM LINE

Core values are a set of beliefs, attitudes, ideals, and practices that are so fundamental as to be a foundation of a leader's actions. Principals and organizations who lead by their core values are more likely to make decisions that align their schools and staff to improvement processes that increase culture measures and job satisfaction. For example, core values are themes such as: integrity, honesty, student support, servant leadership, and respect. Of course, you and your organization may have a different set of them. The list is not as important as the process of collaborating on a common organizational set of values and the implementation of them in the organization's decision-making processes.

In my work, I am careful to use the term values instead of beliefs. Many schools use the terms interchangeably. However, I feel there is a vast distinction between the two terms. The term values implies that a characteristic is unchanging and perpetual. Value means that this characteristic is a long-held principle that becomes a standard of behavior. There is a high level of worth placed on the term. The term belief implies more as a feeling rather than a solid conviction. The connotation is that belief can be temporary or open to change.

SUCCESS INDICATORS

Define 3-5 of your highest priorities and values that clearly articulate what you stand for.

Core values are simple values at the core of who you are as a person and a leader. They are the utmost beliefs that guide you and serve as a filter for your actions. Once identified, they are the benchmarks you use to guide your own decisions, or the decisions your organization makes. One caution, however; limit what you are committed to. By limit I mean prioritize those values into the most important. If you value everything, then nothing is a priority. There is one terrific way to identify whether something is a core value. I always ask if this value is something I am willing to quit my role as principal if I was asked to violate the value. For example, I have fairness as a core value. If my Superintendent ever asked me to violate my sense of fairness for an individual student, would I be willing to leave my role? Absolutely, I would. That means it is a core value to me.

Share your highest priorities with your team and staff.

Once your core values are determined and solidified, communicate them to everyone around you. This level of transparency will assist you in being held accountable to what your beliefs truly are. This accountability will then serve as a baseline for the expectations for yourself and others in the organization. Highly effective professional cultures and collaborative climates are built in this stage. Team members want to serve with leaders who are aligned with their beliefs. Make sure everyone knows what it is you believe.

At the end of each day, debrief your decisions and their alignment with your core values.

To build an effective internal accountability structure, end each day or each team meeting with a short discussion of the alignment of core values and the decisions. Allow for opposition and transparency in the discussion. If you, as the leader, are not congruent with the values stated, then you need to know. This misalignment is what breaks down professional cultures and makes team members no longer want to serve in this organization

EXAMPLE

As a high school principal, I hold my core values as critical components of our schools vision. They are embedded into the fabric of our school. I remember once when I worked with a teacher that acted against many of my core values. My long-held core values are: kindness, integrity, high degree of work ethic, empathy, and fairness. This teacher was unkind to kids. I discussed with her several times the application of her "tough love" philosophy that was void of anything similar to the love component. Additionally, her conversations were inappropriate. She routinely made students feel uneasy by the nature of her stories of other schools she previously worked at. Further, she was unfair to certain students. Her actions toward kids with economic challenges and certain racial makeups was deplorable. As a result, she became a priority for me, my team, and an improvement effort.

In short order, I conducted improvement efforts to improve not only her skill set, but her language and attitude toward students. The efforts were completely aligned with our core values and the

142

stated expectations of the team. By the end of the school year, she had been asked to leave since she was unwilling to accept and act according to our school's core values.

Lead for Win/Win

"Win/win is a belief in the Third Alternative. It's not your way or my way...it's a better way, or the higher way." Stephen Covey

BOTTOM LINE

Highly effective leaders often seek to lead by win/win. The win/win mentality is determined by a leader who seeks to bring a resolution that is advantageous to both parties. It's not always possible, but that is their first goal. Everyone wants to win. If both parties can feel as though they have had a favorable resolution, then we have succeeded. People feel heard in their efforts, supported in their concerns, and ultimately successful. Pursue it. Seek it. Be patient in its pursuit.

SUCCESS INDICATORS

Know your organization's vision deeply.

The first step toward a win/win solution in your organization is to know your vision deeply. Know the vision backward and forward. The vision should be so deeply ingrained into your actions that any step forward is aligned with your vision. Knowing your vision so deeply achieves the basic rule of "combined synergy". Combined synergy is the collaborative effort of everyone in an organization moving toward the same goals and vision at all times. It is very hard to get everyone on the same page. However, shouldn't alignment be an honorable goal to work toward? When goals and efforts are aligned, then parties with rival interests can be closely aligned. As a leader, I can merge the efforts of two groups that have similar interests. Once both groups are unified, then the synergy resulting from their combined efforts brings about "combined synergy".

Is the vision aligned with your core values as a leader?

The vision of an organization should be aligned with the core values of the leader. That congruence should be evident. If it isn't, go back to the fundamental steps of establishing a vision. Seek contributions that are aligned with the values of the leader. This congruence is a given for leaders trying to take an organization to the next level of performance. I hate to use the phrase "it should be a given", but truly if you are a leader who doesn't hold core values similar to the vision of the organization, then a new strategic planning should be undertaken.

Know what a "win" looks like for others.

When determining a win/win opportunity, the leader should know what the elements of a win look like for each member in the situation. If you cannot identify a win, then the target will be infinitely more difficult to hit. Making the positive outcome transparent to both parties will include them in the process of seeking a favorable resolution. Once they know you are seeking a win for them, they'll work with you and not against you.

Be willing to live by your win/win successes.

When a resolution is amenable to more than one party, you should be willing to honor that solution. This solution-seeking collaboration is a higher form of collegiality than we usually see. Honor that agreement by supporting the results in your organization. Use these "wins" as baseline opportunities to set cultural expectations. Your culture can grow in a positive direction depending upon how win/win situations affect them. When teammates actively cheer for one another, a winning attitude results.

144

EXAMPLE

I have had many concerns regarding students' levels of anxiety, overwhelming workload, and lack of sleep. We needed options to bring to bear at Lambert High School. I feel that I exhausted my own ideas and clearly no canned programs offered the solutions we needed. To this end, I went about searching what neighboring schools and schools like our own are doing. This "house hunting" casts a wide net for ideas. I began by listing the concerns I had noticed with students (anxiety, missing assignments, being capable of using downtime, etc.). With this list, I contacted my colleague principals of 11 schools within a 100 mile radius to meet with and discuss what they are doing to address their similar concerns. In my travels, I found that they had very similar concerns. Albeit, we are different schools and organizations, there are certain areas of overlap. They found anxiety and depression sharply on the rise. Additionally, we shared college competition and the concerns of college costs.

We did have one area of divergence for our students. Our initial failure rate at midterm was somewhat consistent with most of the schools visited (averaged 8-10%). We were extremely concerned with that high of a failure rate among our students. However, most of the schools were seemingly unconcerned about their rate. Specifically, if fewer are failing at midterm, then fewer will fail the course at the end of the year. That means more students will be on track for graduation. Our ultimate goal at Lambert High School is to have a 100% graduation rate. I feel that too many schools simply view that goal as unattainable. As principal, I will not accept that line of thinking. Some schools I visited did have good ideas on the area of remediation and support, but I did not see any one school that held all of the strategies that we needed to achieve all of our goals. Our process was long, but became clear.

145

Start with a "What If?" question- One day after searching for the answers to many questions, I said to the administrative team, "Hey guys, I have an idea…". The team realized I had a focused approach and a steely determination. That seemed to scare them when I posed the next "What if" question. I followed up with, "What if we start with a clean slate and build everything toward achieving all of our goals?" With that question I found myself listening to a brisk discussion and collaborative session on details of possible roadblocks. I subsequently stopped everyone and redirected them. "Let's truly think what our dream looks like in actuality. What if our dreams worked on a daily basis? What would our school look like?" The refocusing and conscious decision to plan in an unfettered manner was difficult and yet freeing. Often, we are not able to redefine many of the parameters that guide our work. In this exercise I asked our team to act as if the gloves were taken off. Plan in a truly goal-oriented fashion. The result? It was one of the most remarkable and professional meetings I have ever been a part of. The 10 member team looked at the goals and concerns listed on the board. They thought with a collaborative nature to meet the goals and no other conditions. We filled three pages of notes with possible ideas that could be leveraged to help kids. The guiding question for our next meeting became the mantra for our future discussions and planning. "How can we leverage all of the resources in our control to help kids?" We agreed to take time to think on this question and come back to the table in a week.

Gathering a team together to discuss ideas- One week later, I was afraid the zeal would be lost. I have never been more wrong. The pace at which we planned was frantic. Ideas circled the room like the smoke in the air of a pool hall. We collectively determined that the most impactful resource to leverage was time. "What if we changed the way we used our time?" Of course, time does have an element of constraint in the school business. Buses run with the school system at certain times, kids must be fed each day, number of classes offered, and the length of teacher contracts are factors to consider. We realized that those considerations are immovable. Yet, we chose to consider all the other variables WITHIN the school day.

What targets did I expect for us to meet? In a goal-setting plan, I always sought to establish a metric I wish to attain prior to seeking specific strategies. Consider a metric as an idea parameter to keep us focused toward our own planning.

- How can changing time WITHIN the day positively affect the goals?

- What changes to time are possible?

- Do we have to have a 7 period day?

- Why have we always done lunch the way we are now?

- What does time look like from a student's view?

- What can time look like from a student's view?

Set expected design timeline- With the questions now asked, we needed to gather a lot of information in which to plan further. After a brisk discussion, we delegated roles within the gathering process. This led us to determine how long we would take to return and plan. We agreed to take two weeks to gather information in areas of lunch, number of classes, length of classes, a different schedule, and logistics such as bells. After two weeks, we would return to begin planning.

We brought ideas together. We found few logistics would prevent us from a redesign of time within the school day. With that in mind, we broke into a subcommittee to design a school day that would allow for more time within the day for students. One week later, we came up with a new schedule that eliminated our unique "hybrid" schedule. The "hybrid" schedule entailed a seven class schedule that allowed for three days of seven classes, each comprising 50 minute periods. Then two days allowed for block periods, one day being even periods (2, 4 & 6) and the other being off periods (1, 3, 5 & 7). The even day also contained an Instructional Focus (IF) class that allowed for remediation and other options. However, in the 5 years we held IF, it never materialized into an effective course. Rather, it was difficult to manage and never had "belief in" from students or staff. The new schedule being proposed was an elimination of the block days and a straight lunch with optional time for kids and teachers. We saw this as the answer we were researching for. The schedule, called Plan A, seemingly met all of the questions we posed.

To focus our discussions we held the Plan A schedule up to our "movable and non-movable" forces. Does this new schedule negatively affect the bus schedules, teachers contracts, logistics, and classes? It appeared to meet all of the criteria we had set. Could we have found the answer we needed? It was time to take our Plan A to a larger team of players. Our Leadership Team at Lambert High School is composed of a department chair for each academic department as well as critical staff within the school. The team is made up of twenty members. I felt they needed to join the team to give us full perspective. What follows is one of the biggest surprises and learning opportunities I have ever experienced. When we proudly presented every aspect of the new "Lunch & Learn" plan, we were shocked with the reception. There was at least four minutes of dead silence. I tried to assess the looks on my colleagues' faces. They were not happy. Apparently, we missed something. Were we dead in the water? Are we not moving toward helping the kids and staff?

The possible new plan that we were so proud of was failing. We had three choices at this point: One, we could get defensive, frustrated, and push the flawed plan without any regard to our colleagues' opinions. Two, we could discard that plan entirely and keep with the status quo. Or, three, we could elicit their feedback and go back to the drawing board. In a momentary decision, my learning and professional direction was solidified. I asked for their honest opinions and detailed feedback in an attempt to construct a final product that met everyone's goals. We asked what elements missed their mark or what they were we not seeing. It was evident that we did not understand how much the science and fine arts departments needed the block classes. They felt they were immovable factors to meet kids' needs within their classes. The entire Leadership and Administrative Team agreed that we could not move forward with any plan that left a group behind. I was so proud of our team. This was a true sign of the "Belief In" philosophy I had been seeking for so long.

Missing the Mark- It appears that missing the mark had led us back to the drawing board with a new charge. Our charge was clear: construct a plan with all of the same criteria as before but also keep the block classes that were needed for kids in the science and fine arts classes. As further confirmation, I asked my Principal's Student Advisory Class to give feedback on the plan. They added one more factor to consider. They asked that any plan not allow for athletic teams, clubs, or the band to be able to meet during this time. Their feeling was that the focus of student time would be lost if allowed to meet with groups in this fashion. Thus, we'd been missing one criteria we set.

A colleague and I were standing in the hall one morning. As we were talking we found ourselves struggling with a new plan. I asked her, "What if…we added a class?" We looked at each other for what felt like, two full minutes… Since she and I knew each other very well, she knew where I was going with this question. She looked at me and said, "I think I know…" We ran to my office, took out some scrap paper and doodled for a silent five minutes. In that time, we exchanged ideas and doodles several times. She would write, then I would scribble to add to it. Finally, we were on the track. In an effort to save the block classes and maximize time for kids, we drew up a new concept. Our seven academic classes each day, with no block classes, became seven academic classes, three days and two days of block classes, with a scheduled class period for lunch (an eight period). The lunch periods for kids would remain the same each and every day. This allowed for two days of block classes to remain and a daily consistency that students wanted. In our doodling haze, we scratched out the format and both cried in exuberance. It appeared as though we had it. I used the radio to call for a few more members of our team to come in and look at it for mistakes. It appeared to hit the targets to them as well. To double check, I went to the Fine Arts and Science department chairs' classrooms to show them our creation. They both smiled and gave a hearty thumbs up.

In an effort to triple check our efforts, we asked a few of the "nay-sayers" to check our concept. A true Polaroid moment in my mind followed. They agreed and approved. Not only had it worked, but the process was a true learning moment for us all. Newer members of my administrative team saw the value of collaboration and determination. Longtime veterans were astounded by the effects of target-guided collaboration in the development of Lunch & Learn. Now that we had a solid plan for Lunch & Learn created, I sought feedback from my principal colleagues within my own school system. I asked for their feedback to help spotlight any missing details we had not considered. It was audacious, but doable. They were not eager to try such a plan until they saw it in operation.

The new Lunch & Learn plan required a tremendous amount from administrators, secretaries, counselors, custodians, food service, and the facility. We had to create new norms and processes for adults taking lunch and break times. All staff unencumbered during Lunch & Learn were to be available at all times to assist students. No one was allowed to lunch or meet during this time. Considering that 1500 students would be in the halls, courtyards, lunchroom, and media center at the same time it would require a new norm for custodial and clean up crews. Counselors would now be available for the entire period. Administrators also had to be available for supervision to allow for teachers to support kids.

This new program called" Lunch & Learn" truly benefited all of our groups. It benefitted students (more wellness and homework time), staff (more support and planning time), and the school (improved academic and wellness culture). It was intentional. Truly, a win/win/win result.

Lead for "Belief In"

"A believer... is never disturbed because other persons do not see the fact which he sees." Ralph Waldo Emerson

BOTTOM LINE

Many school leaders seek growth, improvement, and collaboration. They often call this level of commitment "buy in". However, I don't think that "buy in" commitment is enough. Elite leaders seek a "belief-in" commitment from team members to reach greater heights of growth, improvements, and collaboration. "Belief- in" is an elite-level commitment where team members identify the team's success as their success. They only feel as though they are successful when the team has succeeded. Team members tend to forego their own success in lieu of the organization's success. They want everyone in the organization to win from their contributions. I call it a "bone deep" commitment.

SUCCESS INDICATORS

Show teammates what further commitment looks like.

As a leader of an organization, modeling behavior is a very common way to display and reinforce behaviors that we expect to see replicated. When it comes to deeper levels of commitment, going "all in" with our own commitment is expected. However, we intend for the replication of this behavior in others. As an example, we can display the "belief in" standard of commitment by our own value of the organization achieving. When a teacher has an exceptionally good result on an assessment, we can value the gains as our gains. Conversely, owning the lack of achievement is also a form of "belief in". We, as leaders, only win as the organization wins. If we model this behavior, team members will understand that the individual is important, but the success of the organization is valued as primary.

I like the term that National Championship winning coach, Kirby Smart used to his players to reinforce the concept of "belief in". He didn't use this term, but his term meant so much to so many people. He used "Keep Chopping" as a way of indicating to his players and fans to keep progressing forward. When the team wins, they win.

Acknowledge the costs of "belief-in" with their further commitment.

There is a cost to a greater depth or level of commitment to the individuals in the organization. Linking your success to the success of an organization can feel a bit hollow unless you are completely ready. The success of an organization can be slower than that of an individual. It takes time for us all to improve and see those gains or results. For the results of an individual, gains can come quite quickly. Deferring success for that of the organization can be a waiting game. One must be ready and supported in this waiting game. As the leader, we are obligated to support team members in this duration. We can do so by giving constant encouragement and descriptive feedback to the individuals in the interim before the organization shows results.

Appreciate them and their gifts for the team's success.

Leaders celebrate their team member's successes as a team wins. When an individual does something beyond the expectations they link it to the organization's gain. Of course, organizations have a life of their own, but they are also a conglomeration of individuals and their successes and losses. I often use the phrase "Together we can and will succeed".

Include them on team decisions and movements.

One attribute of team member's commitment being at the level of "belief in" is that they need to be included in decision-making and setting direction for the organization. They are highly committed and involved, so great leaders value team members and their influence on the organization. This is the least we can do for team members as they are fully committed. To include them and not ask for this level of commitment is leaving influence on the table. We cannot optimally grow as an organization if these two attributes are not aligned. Additionally, it values team member's at the highest level if we are partners with them as they have partnered with us. Those with deeper commitment deserve this level of involvement.

Love them at every opportunity.

Team members who demonstrate that they are committed at such a high level deserve a true partnership to value their commitment. Their commitment is a gift to the organization. It is highly regarded and valued. This level of commitment is invaluable to the growth of an organization. For a large organization to operate at its highest level of effectiveness, there needs to be a core of individuals who are this committed. Their time, commitment, and investment are a treasure to your organization's success. You, as the leader, should reciprocate for them how much you value their commitment by giving continually to them.

EXAMPLE

"Belief-in vs. Buy-in vs. Interest-in"- These three levels of operational ownership can determine a person's ability to commit to the overall needs of the team or organization. As Principal, I use this information to know my staff well in regards to their perspectives toward the change process and their commitment to the organization. Of course, there are degrees to each and that combination allows me to find the right location in the organization for each staff member to maximize their abilities, motivations, and their willingness for contributions. For instance, when beginning a new student support initiative that would substantially change the school schedule, I knew that certain staff members were best suited to be on the development team (Belief-in) and others on implementation (Buy-in). Albeit, some staff were simply along for the ride (Interest-in) given their lack of perspective toward such a substantial change and their operational commitment toward the organization. In the end, the decisions regarding perspectives and commitment paid huge dividends in the effectiveness of these change initiatives. These team members that were Belief-in people, drove home the initiatives and led us to greater heights. As a leader, seek those people out and align them toward your organizational goals.

Lead with Innovation

"Innovation means acting like a scientist. Dream, plan, try, fail, try again, and so on..." Gary Davison

BOTTOM LINE

Great leaders who want their organizations to succeed aim high and use the best available methods to obtain positive results. Rarely do leaders aim to be innovative for the sake of being different. However, when circumstances allow for a new method or a new manner of working, innovation becomes a valuable strategy to employ. Innovative outcomes should be led with the conditions of innovation. Setting the conditions for innovation are simple. Trust, accountability, new learnings, feedback, and reflection all are valuable skills leaders use to enable them to be innovative in the moment. There will be many times that we fail. In those moments, leaders act as if they were scientists. They try, reflect, fail, try again, fail, try yet again, reflect and document what worked and why. This process is simply known as being innovative. New ideas and applications are not a single act upon themselves. They are the result of planning and acting in a new way.

SUCCESS INDICATORS

Innovation begins well before the project starts.

Innovation is a result of well planned out steps and intentions on behalf of the team or organization. It starts with being open to new thoughts, ideas, and processes. Innovation is rarely a blueprint or recipe that is easily followed or a step-by-step menu. Intentional planning, budgeting, allocation of resources, and professional learning are all components to being innovative. Once a problem is posed to be solved, leaders use their experience and reflection to gather the best strategies to solve the problem. However, when there is a new problem or a circumstance where the best available methods are not possible, innovative thinking begins. Here is where leaders use planning to start the process for innovative thinking and the execution of innovative strategies.

Always ask questions.

Innovative leaders are led by asking questions. They know where they hope to be in terms of results. However, they may not know exactly what the steps are to accomplish this goal. When being innovative, they are open to trying new approaches to beginning the work. Usually the best way to start the process is to ask questions of yourself and the team. "What if?" is usually the best approach to beginning the discussions of using innovative thought. Follow that question up with a list of questions to give your team a set of information to use as a baseline. This approach is called the "8-year-old questioning method". Approach the work with your team by asking questions as if you were an 8-year-old looking at something you have never seen before. "What is that? Why can't we? How can we? What if we try this?" are all examples of the 8-year-old questioning method. The method also emphasizes the curiosity of the young and the collaboration of others. Primary questions are disarming to others and basic enough for everyone to engage.

Align resources.

When an organization is operating in an innovative manner, a leader must align the resources. Aligning resources to support the team members in the organization gives them the necessary tools to accomplish the development of new ways of operating, new strategies, and new elements of the culture. Time, budget, and collaboration are resources that can be aligned to assist in the development of innovation. The purpose of aligning resources is to allow for slowing down, asking questions, and exploring possibilities.

Reward creative outcomes and those who try.

Leaders of an organization have the ability to encourage or discourage certain behaviors. Great leaders should encourage innovative thinking and processes. Encouragement can be generated through the feedback given to team members. When asking questions, leaders can give credit and support to the team by alluding to aspects that meet the team's needs. They can also be rewarded with resources such as time, budgetary consideration, and support as a result of innovative practices. Rewards can also be given for the attempts toward innovation as a way to reinforce a new culture.

Lead for autonomy.

To lead an innovative culture among members of your team, leaders need to be comfortable with not being comfortable. Not being comfortable means that moving a large organization into the decision-making and planning phase requires a new level of trust and autonomy. Setting the conditions for innovation allows leaders to have their team members closer to the decision-making plans than ever before. Trust and feedback are critical at this juncture. Without trust and feedback, autonomy is close to negligence. However, once trust is clearly developed on a team, autonomy can serve as the glue that allows creativity to bind team members together. Once planning is moving forward, use feedback and reflection to guide the next steps of development. Once these are in high gear, the culture will match the goal of the task you are trying to achieve.

EXAMPLE

Dr. Tim Elmore, respected Education Futurist and Author, recently called Lambert High School's Lunch & Learn program a "remarkable innovation" in his National Leadership Conference on June 20, 2019. Once I received verification from such an accomplished and admired colleague that our attempt at a unique solution to solve one of our problems, our confidence to call ourselves innovative was achieved. Of course, you are reading the process I have since called a "Win-ovation". The win (staff)-win (students)-win (community & parents) of Lunch & Learn and the process used in its design have reinforced the elements of Win-ovation.

Innovation is not a new concept. Business leaders, speakers, and writers all have been touting the benefits of innovation. They claim that the work culture benefits. However, much of what is heralded as innovative is just a shiny new wrapper on an old concept. This could not be further from our story of innovation. Rather than setting out to "innovate"; we sought to solve a problem. The result has been heralded by many as innovative. Here, we detail our story of solving a problem. One cannot call themselves innovators. That is left for the audience to determine. If someone calls themselves innovators or seeks to sell you an innovative strategy... Beware! They should tell you that the results of solving a problem led to processes that were later called innovative. Only time will tell what is innovative and what is simply repackaging the same processes. Innovation is not a destination, rather it is a journey. Innovators seek to solve problems and arrive at the destination. The problem we sought to solve was: "What can we do to help kids learn more effectively, diffuse some of the stressors they are currently feeling, and alleviate growing concerns from teachers about their own profession?" The innovation we became known for was the connection between our problem ("What can we do to help kids learn more effectively, diffuse some of the stressors they are currently feeling, and alleviate growing concerns from teachers about their own profession?") and the solution (rearranging our greatest resource of time to meet these needs). The uniqueness of the path is the connection between the problem and solution. Finally, the unique solution met everyone's goals. We rearranged our resources to give kids and teachers more time and the school accomplished increased support structures within the school day.

Lead Just Out of Your Reach

"If your actions inspire others to dream more, learn more, do more, and become more... You are a leader." John Quincy Adams

BOTTOM LINE

What does success mean to you? Are you satisfied with simply meeting a minimum standard? Are you comfortable with being average? Great leaders are never content with merely meeting a mediocre standard. Great leaders search for the unattainable. They strive to get better each and every day. They are relentless in their passion for excellence. Leading just out of your reach is about setting goals that would be considered audacious by many. They seek to attain perfection and will "settle" for excellence. Set a mark just ahead of that standard and then go after it, relentlessly.

SUCCESS INDICATORS

Know your own abilities and limitations.

As a leader in an organization that values learning and growing, leaders must be fully aware of their own assets and liabilities. Before a leader can seek to attain a higher standard than merely average, they must be aware of what skills are considered strengths and weaknesses for them. To seek a greater level, starting with your own skill set is a must. Once a leader is aware, then they can delve into what they can do to grow toward excellence in their skills.

Define success for you, your organization, and team members.

When there is not a common vision of what success looks like in an organization, the standard tends to become average performance. However, if you are seeking excellence as the performance standard for your organization, then the standard needs to be intentionally set. Collaboratively discuss what an excellent result would look like. Then, as a team, work to identify strategies and methods to attain this new standard. Once it is attained, the new average will become an excellence standard.

Collaboratively set benchmarks as a team that are out of your reach.

Once the result measure has been set, defining the process for attaining such a goal is necessary. The use of benchmarks to delineate the steps to be taken are critical. These new benchmarks will serve as the new process performance measure and the result measure will be a confirmation measure. Great leaders lead through monitoring the process their team uses to work on a daily basis. The results will come if the processes are performed with fidelity. The organization can start using the term "success indicators" to identify benchmarks of a successful process.

Start moving toward the new success indicators.

Organizations that are constantly using feedback with success indicators consider winning as a mere result of superior planning and solid use of feedback to drive elements of their process. Success indicators are used as small interval indicators of alignment toward the vision of the organization.

EXAMPLE (Personal application)

In my early teaching, I used to call my new perspective, *Commitment to Excellence*. I pledged to my students that I'd give them my best effort every day. I incentivized them in holding me to my words. I offered points to anyone who found me not giving my all to any effort we did in class. Additionally, *"Commitment to Excellence"* became my class' mantra. It was written at the top of every paper we did for homework, notes, tests, etc. It meant that the creator of whatever was done is pledging to give their very best effort. I made signs and placed them all over the school. We even shortened it to *"C2E"*. It became our secret from the rest of the school. It became our jet fuel to greater achievement. Their commitment was "belief in" and not merely "buy in".

Personally, I embraced the new perspective and found a new name for it. "What's Next?" Became a perspective and personal philosophy all wrapped up together. The perspective of chasing excellence has been a hallmark of my professional career and personal life. I find myself constantly not being satisfied when a moderate goal is achieved. A lofty goal can become a moderate goal once it is surpassed. For example, I always wanted to earn a black belt in karate. It took years of practice and dedication, but Master Glen Smith honored me with my first black belt. Once earned, I began to refine my skills and that led me to pursue Krav Maga. Again, years of practice led me to earn my level five certification. After years of hand to hand combat training, it took me into boxing. As a 50-year-old man, I found that combat sports were taking a physical toll on me. I switched endeavors. For the past years, I have set my sights on Obstacle Course Racing. Essentially, it is trail running with obstacles interspersed to make for a challenge like I have never found. Upon completion of a race, where I find myself to be possibly the oldest competitor, I feel a sense of satisfaction and pride. I allow myself that feeling as a reward. As the medals hang on my wall the joy is quickly absorbed, and turned to the next race. The process I use to prioritize goals, set matrices, give and receive feedback, and assess the inertia needed to continue on long goals are only a few of the skills needed to push beyond being pleased and satisfied in the moment. Once absorbed, the moment is gone and excellence is, once again, being chased.

My "What's Next?" perspective has set the stage for the largest endeavors of my life. Several years ago, it was an honor to be asked to open a brand-new high school serving as its first principal. I took my "What's Next?" attitude and began to plan for the new school. Setting vision, establishing teams, facilitating discussions around culture, processes, and traditions, fascinated me. For the past 14 years, our organization has been a model school for top-notch academics, state and national championship athletics, as well as innovative student support structures. We are very proud of the teamwork that resulted. The process that we have relied on has, in my humble opinion, been the difference-maker for us as an exemplary school.

PART 5:
Planning and Execution

Highly effective leaders garner great success with planning and execution. Planning involves forward thinking with action steps aligned to success indicators. Execution involves being intentional about applying the plans. Great leaders are adept at this skill through numerous opportunities to practice and thorough feedback. However, execution can be difficult for aspiring leaders as they can be slow to begin or meek in their delivery. In this section, these skills are spelled out in detail to allow for aspiring leaders to gain an understanding of the elements needed to be successful in execution and decision-making. Leaders wishing to grow other leaders should use trust as a crutch to allow aspiring leaders to attempt, make mistakes, and attempt again. Of course, feedback is critical to their development and the trust generated between leader and aspiring leader will pay dividends for the organization.

Lead by Communication

"The art of communication is the language of leadership." James Humes

BOTTOM LINE

Communication is the lifeblood of high-powered leadership. Elite leaders are master communicators. They are capable of using sophisticated communication strategies and eliciting actions and responses to their words. Remember the analogy about the tree in the woods? Well, as legend asks, if a tree falls in the woods and there is no one there to hear it, did it make a noise? Philosophers and wise people for eternity have questioned this riddle. Many have said yes, there was a noise even though it wasn't heard. Others questioned if the area is devoid of a receiver of the sound, was it a completed loop? They tend to say not. Regardless of your stance, the tree in the woods analogy is appropriate for leadership. Instead of a tree falling , we are focusing on whether a follower has understood a directive given by the leader. If it is given, but not understood, did it occur? Is it only valid if it was heard, understood, and followed up?

I wish to give another perspective on this analogy and subsequent question. It doesn't matter how it's given. If it isn't understood, then you're dead in the water as a leader. For elite-level leadership to occur, leaders must be aware that their words, actions, and intentions have consequences. It is incumbent upon leaders to be certain they are communicating in a manner that is heard, understood, and easily adapted. The flexibility of the leaders is vital to be fully understood.

SUCCESS INDICATORS

Assess your own communication abilities… Be honest.

Elite leaders know they are effective communicators. However, what about those emerging or novice leaders? How do they grow into master communicators? First, they need to know their own strengths and weaknesses as communicators. Effective leaders are keenly aware that they have to be highly skilled orators and speechmakers. Not all speaking opportunities are in front of large crowds, most is done in small groups or individually. However, the spoken word is a tremendous opportunity to influence team members to achieve the goals of the team. The written word is incredibly important to the leader as well. However, different opportunities for influence are found with the written word. Letters, emails, text messages, and social media posts are used by leaders as tools. Regardless of which mode is chosen, leaders need to be fully aware of the strengths they possess as well as the weaknesses in their ability to communicate effectively. Once a strength is made aware of them, elite-level leaders continue to develop their skills. The best communicators never rely on those skills. They are always seeking to improve them, even if they are strengths. Weaknesses are given a much higher priority as communication is an incredibly important skill for any leader. Books, tape series, videos, and workshops are given to aid those in need to help in developing strong communication skills. I prefer to place aspiring leaders in opportunities to use spoken language and then give them actionable, descriptive feedback.

Know your team member's communication and how to best reach them.

Again, the importance of communication strengths cannot be overstated. However, for your team members, there are many protocols to determine communication styles and strengths. However, I would rely on the "ear test". I use the ear test to help me determine if a potential leader is skilled at communication. I give them a task that involves planning, staging various timelines and elements, as well as follow up decisions. I then ask them to talk me through it. If they can summarize effectively and then elaborate to include all the necessary details, they are equipped to begin training as a leader. Once they demonstrate proficiency, I will give constant feedback on the effectiveness of their communication strategies as well as the content communicated.

No, it's not fair, it doesn't have to be fair.

Each leader and team member will have different strengths, different weaknesses, and various needs in their skill set development. No, it isn't fair that some will require more work than others. However, it is the leader's responsibility to assist others in the growth of their communication skills. There are some leaders that may seem to be naturally gifted at public speaking or written communications. However, work must be put in to improve their skill sets to the most effective level we can each reach. A failure of communication is a failure of leadership.

Surround yourself with others not like you.

For robust discussion and the growth of skill sets, elite leaders surround themselves with communicators that do not share their same strengths. This method of collaborative peer improvement works in the area of communication skills. Some teams will have a tremendous writer. Others may possess that public speaker that has audiences eating out of their hand. Whatever the case, aligning your team with a variety of communication abilities and levels can enhance the effectiveness of any team.

EXAMPLE

I remember I once had a member of my executive team in a large high school. She had tremendous leadership potential but needed guidance. She was a dynamo but would communicate in such a way that her audience would get lost with too many words being used. Her concepts were clear and well thought out, but the volume of words and the speed at which she shared them made it difficult for listeners to keep up with her as well as understand all of the concepts. This leader was incredibly intelligent and well spoken, however she needed to brush up on skills to be highly effective and elite in her communications. As a leader, I had to get her to prioritize her language to be more effective.

As the weeks and months progressed, I worked closely with her on her communication strategies. Reminders of the audience and their perspective were reminders to slow down, assess the levels of understanding, and the needs they had as listeners. It took a few hard conversations, a lot of follow-up, and some direct actions (use bullet points, word limit, etc.) to help her. In the end, all of the detailed work paid off. She is a wonderful, highly effective principal today.

Lead by Setting the Conditions for Success

"A leader's job is clear. You set the conditions for success and give feedback toward those conditions." Gary Davison

BOTTOM LINE

Great leaders operate from a detailed and well thought-out plan. They are intentionally influential with their team members and constituents. Their influence is designed to affect more than merely the results or achievements. The highly effective leaders focus their intentions on the processes aligned for the desired results they are hoping to attain. Additionally, leaders are responsible for aligning the necessary resources for their teams to succeed. This alignment of successful strategies and processes to resources is called 'Setting the Conditions for Success'. Finally, a leader's job is to establish benchmarks are the critical elements for setting the conditions for success.

SUCCESS INDICATORS

Determine the organization's vision.

Great leaders develop the targets for their organizations from the vision established. Subsequently, they will determine benchmarks along the way to achieving the vision. These steps are used in Setting the Conditions for Success by giving leaders and their team members targets to aim at. Great leadership is always contingent upon having a direction and an aspirational destination. Great leaders are never floating in the direction of accidental outcomes. Intentionality is determined by a dictated path.

Align the organization's processes toward that vision.

In great learning organizations the processes that generate success for students are all aligned with the vision. Each process is accompanied by standards and expectations for each member of the team. Examples of these processes are: student support, culture, recognitions, instruction and assessment, etc. These processes are essential to the mission and vision of the organization. However, alignment is critical.

Establish benchmarks for success.

Great leaders often have a good idea of the effectiveness of their organizations. However, they do not settle for the feeling of success. They are directed by the use of benchmarks to determine periodical success toward the accomplishment of small, periodic goals along the way to achieving the stated vision of the organization. Moreover, any effort that is not aligned with their benchmarks will cause an organization to flounder in poor processes, thus missing any goals set.

Provide resources necessary for success.

Setting the Conditions for Success of any organization requires the alignment of resources necessary to accomplish the goals. Of course, unlimited resources are not a reality for anyone. Great leaders are able to balance current resource needs with the availability of resources at hand. Additionally, they are able to assess allocations for future resources. Budgetary considerations, time allocation, and the use of personnel are key aspects of leaders Setting the Conditions for Success.

Discuss your focus for feedback on the alignment toward your vision.

Once leaders have Set the Conditions for Success, they will give objective, descriptive feedback to anyone and everyone in the organization toward the vision. This feedback is done in accord with the elements of feedback listed previously in this book. Leaders grow and organizations flourish by being aligned toward their vision.

EXAMPLE

In my 22 years as a principal and the high school and elementary school levels, I have spent the majority of my career Setting the Condition for Success and then providing feedback on those conditions. As an organization, we have prioritized student support as a non-negotiable factor for us. The vision of our school as well as the processes and policies of our school are built around the concept of student support. High achieving students as well as students struggling in their courses all have the same access to support strategies and structures. There is a lunch program that allows for students to have an hour for eating, completing homework, studying, or working on projects. This additional time has benefitted students of all ability levels. In addition to eating and work time, students are encouraged to rest, catch their breath, and seek wellness activities to make a long day a little shorter.

As the leader of the organization, I used many strategies to Set the Conditions for Success by aligning our greatest resource, time, to the greatest need and the vision of the school...student support! Additionally, budgetary allocations and personnel are prioritized for the same goals. Each day, I analyze and assess these conditions being allocated for their alignment toward the goals and the likelihood for effectiveness. To that end, my job is to align all of these factors toward achieving that vision. Our budget, master schedule, and hiring are focused on that goal.

Lead through Visibility

"The more you can be seen and be present with people, the more they will trust you." Gary Davison

BOTTOM LINE

As a Principal, we can add value to our leadership if we are visible. Visibility is not merely being seen. Interaction, trust, and empathy are key elements to the truly visible leader. Team members know they are cared for, trusted, and known by the leader. Being present at events, in classrooms, and around your school and community are demonstrative acts that show others you are interested in them and their efforts. Additionally, being visible means the leader's actions are synonymous and in alignment with the values of the organization. This transparency confirms the trust that leaders seek in their team members. The resulting confidence contributes mightily to an effective school culture. This culture will support your actions and language.

SUCCESS INDICATORS

Be the one who welcomes people each day!

There are several actions leaders can take to indicate they are visible and highly interested in supporting members of their team. It is a small effort, but the resulting trust and confidence is an exponential benefit. So worthy of dedicated time, that every leader should employ this in their skill set. To smile, welcome each person by name, and wish them a good day exudes caring, empathy, and sets the tone for a pleasant day. This baseline to begin each day establishes your openness, calmness, and trustworthiness. Find a manner that works for you and employ it each day. Lead the organization into a great day, each day!

Look students/staff in the eye and not through them.

As you talk to team members, students, and community members intentionally look each of them in the eye as you speak to them. This connection establishes the trust you need to have as a leader to be influential in the organization. A face to face connection ensures that you will have a better chance of effective communications. Avoid glancing and looking through them in conversations. People are aware when a leader is looking in an obligatory manner and not concentrating on the conversation. Be authentic and honest in your discussions with others.

Knowing the names of students and all members of your team is a highly effective manner of connecting with them. As a leader, you have the obligation to know people's names and use it in discussing with them. This small action adds to the confidence, transparency, and connection that you establish with them. Take a yearbook and use it to study students' names over the summer, prior to them coming back to school in the Fall. Be prepared and you will reap huge benefits from this consideration.

Go to events and enjoy yourself.

Leadership and management of large organizations are fraught with time commitments and dedicated portions of the day that the leader is encumbered. However your time is spent, these are opportunities to engage with your communities and teams that cannot be missed. In a high school, for instance, there are at least 20 sports teams, many fine arts events, and academic opportunities that can be the setting for a leader's visibility and connection. Students, parents, and staff enjoy interacting with the leader in these low pressure events. While at these events let others see you enjoying yourself as you support those in your sphere of influence. Be seen by as many people as possible. Shake a few hands, ask questions of others, and get to know people who are not comfortable walking into schools. This may be your best opportunity to connect with many people.

Schedule visibility into your day.

Highly effective leaders are intentional about how they spend their time. Detailed blocks of time are dedicated in their calendars. The adage about a checkbook holds here. It was said if you look into someone's checkbook, it will show you where their priorities lie. In the world of a leader, if you were to look at their daily calendar, you can see clearly where their priorities lie. This look at their calendar shows the time spent on important items rather than playing catch up on urgent things. Time blocks are placed intentionally into the schedule rather than just following the flow of the day. If leaders merely follow the flow of the day, urgency will trump importance every time. Don't get stuck in this trap. Leaders need this intentional dedication rather than fluttering around from thing to thing. Focus on goals, people, and commitments to growth.

Make a plan for your visibility opportunities. A wonderful strategy is to take your blank schedule and place daily opportunities to "set the conditions for success", take "feedback walks", and "speaking tours" to focus on interactions in your daily schedule. When meetings and other things need to be scheduled, place them around dedicated blocks as they are priorities. The resulting efficiency will help a leader's effectiveness in building trust and an effective culture.

EXAMPLE

As the leader of a large suburban high school, I found a location on our campus that has the highest visibility and provides the best opportunity to talk to students and staff. This became a major priority as I wished to maximize visibility among those two important groups. In addition to being visible, I wanted to be able to conduct "school business" as needed with staff and with kids. For example, on an average Wednesday morning, I was able to have 12 brief follow up student conversations regarding a variety of topics. These conversations revolved around recommendation letters, performance at the volleyball match from the previous night, preparing for the upcoming school play, the development of a new student club, and asking how the older sibling of a current student was faring in college. The 8 staff conversations were around leave requests, professional learning events upcoming, as well as an upcoming football game that was critical to our season. This intentional location has served me very well. There are three major entrances to our school for students and staff. To the left, students driving themselves enter the building. To the right, students who take the bus to school enter the building. Finally coming in straight to the area are students who are dropped off by parents. The convergence of these three areas makes this a prime location to be seen and be able to interact with everyone that is in the building at the time. Each morning I gladly greet and smile for each and every student and staff member that comes by. It is my time to attempt to "out nice" everyone I meet. This strategy has been in place for 15 years and has become a tradition in the school. When I am away at a meeting, another member of the staff will casually step in to take the duty.

Lead by Choosing "Effective vs. Efficient"

"To build greatness, go for effective, not efficient, until it is a time crunch. Then, balance between effective and efficient." Gary Davison

BOTTOM LINE

Highly effective Principals know when to prioritize elements of effectiveness and efficiency. These are vastly different concepts and one that needs to be focused and used with intentionality. There are definitive opportunities to focus on each one. Effectiveness is concerned with quality, commitment, results, and outcomes. Efficiency is more concerned with time, process, and quantity. As a leader there are moments to prioritize your efforts in each direction. Effectiveness is used by leaders as a result of solid planning and procedures. Brainstorming, Socratic discussions, collaboration, and long-term strategic planning are examples of leaders focusing on effectiveness. Time on task, fire drills, lockdown procedures, and accomplishing large quantities of work are examples of leaders focusing on efficiency. Moreover, there are many other examples of each concentration. Great leaders know which to focus with and how to employ these for the benefit of their teams.

SUCCESS INDICATORS

Let's be clear... Emergencies need efficient action!

There is no disagreement from myself or any other highly effective leader that emergency situations rely heavily on the ability for the leader to focus on efficiency in the moment. When time is of the essence, a leader seeking efficiency is critical and will produce the most advantageous results. Such circumstances are: fire drills, "real" lockdown scenarios, a social media threat situation, a student who is injured, or even moving a large number of students to a safety drill. However, emergencies are of a higher degree of priority.

Importance of accountability brings effectiveness into play.

When elite leaders are providing feedback for the purposes of accountability, time is a consideration. Rather taking a suitable amount of time for the effort is critical. Moving slower for the learner can help their retention and understanding. Remember that effectiveness is an area where learning will occur. Once a learned strategy becomes understood, the speed at which it occurs can increase. However, the adage, "Start slow to go fast" is relevant in this phase.

Focusing on people brings effectiveness into play.

174

Wellness, staff retention, and social emotional needs of the adults in the organization certainly means that a leader should focus on quality rather than speed. This means that effectiveness is the primary emphasis. Once a system or process becomes ingrained into the fabric of the organization, speed of the application can be increased. Thus, it can then be an efficiency focus. People will always remember how they are treated by their leaders. Subsequently, take your time and treat it as an area of focus. Take your time to get it right. You will always gain credibility and respect from your teams if you focus on quality.

Speed is a clear indicator of what you employ when.

As a leader focusing on being highly effective in everything you do, consider what speed you need to decide or act. This is the primary determiner as to which focus you will have as the leader. If you, as the leader, act in a triage manner, then efficiency will be the primary focus. Triage indicates that you must act quickly. Then debrief to become more effective after the action. For example, if a student was hurt, act quickly to get them assistance then determine how effective your processes were. Conversely, if you are planning a long term action, act deliberately with effectiveness being the primary focus. Speed can increase after idea generation, processes are improved, and methods of assessing success are determined.

Debrief both circumstances with your team.

Whether you are acting with an effectiveness or efficiency focus, great leaders determine methods to assess their effectiveness after the action. In this mode, highly effective leaders debrief with their teams to improve commitment, focus, quality, and ownership. This step is as important as any other step. Do not ever skip this step.

EXAMPLE

Early in my career as a principal, I ran into a crucial conversation regarding a program and staffing consideration. I was asked to open a brand new high school. It was an honor and I had a tremendous amount of work to do to meet the needs of the community. The new school was built with a million-dollar Culinary Arts laboratory. Early in the 2000's this level of food service was an emerging desire of many kids, families, and the industry at large. As I began staffing for the long term success of the school, I needed to prioritize quality over speed in staffing for this position. Knowing that this pathway would have only one teacher for many years, I wanted to make sure the level of quality was attained and determined to take my time to get this hire right.

After many months of interviewing over 20 candidates, I was unable to find the right fit for our school, program, and the needs of the community. The perfect candidate was not found and we opened the school without the position being filled. In our first year, I refused to open this premier program. Not only were people disappointed, but there was substantial discussion at the school system level and the community level. I had to answer my process and goal for this hire. The second year came and went. Again, no teacher for this million dollar program.

In the Spring of the second year, I was conducting a national search for the right person to open this program. Seemingly unrelated, I was contacted by a local church to help them interview for their senior pastor position. Seemingly unconnected to any needs we had at school, I thought this would be a great way to support our community. As I met their leading candidate, he and his family came to our school. During our meeting with the family, I was taken aback by the name of the lead candidate's wife. It sounded incredibly familiar. Interestingly enough, her name was one of the candidates that I identified in our national search for this

Culinary Arts position. During our discussion, I learned that she was the very same teacher I had been searching for weeks before. So, I interviewed her on the spot. It was very serendipitous. She was perfect for the role. Her husband was hired as the senior pastor and I hired her as the Director of Culinary Arts.

Waiting to hire a teacher for this position was hard, but very necessary. Effectiveness was the goal of the hire. I could have merely hired one of the candidates we met with prior. However, there would have always been a concern that we didn't find the right person. Since then, this teacher was named Teacher of the Year, built an incredible program, and has inspired many students to follow her into the field of Culinary Arts at the post-secondary level. It was a real win. After all the dust settled, I debriefed the process with my team. I found ways that I could have acted a little more efficiently in the process, but waiting for quality was the key to our success. Steadfast determination was the key quality to begin the program.

Lead with Alignment

"If everyone is moving forward together, then success takes care of itself." Henry Ford

BOTTOM LINE

Highly effective leaders seek to lead their organizations to success as measured by the indicators named in their vision and goals. Visionary alignment means all members of your team are working toward a common vision and actions measured by indicators that are aligned with this vision. Attaining alignment can create synergy with team members, students, and the community. Align all of the factors necessary to succeed. Consider everything when planning.

SUCCESS INDICATORS

Share the vision of the organization with all of your constituents.

Highly effective leaders have a constant eye to the direction of the organization. Close examination should be shared with everyone to align their efforts, commitment, and processes with the goals. As a leader, you should communicate and sell the vision at all times. It is deeply ingrained into all of your conversations, feedback, and encouragement. The more a leader replicates the vision in their discussions, the likelihood that the vision will become actions in the organization.

Discuss each person's role within the vision.

As great leaders give feedback, they use the vision to frame their efforts of descriptive and objective feedback to members of their teams. The vision is the context for all discussions. This will emphasize the importance of the vision and each member's influence and participation in the achievement of the vision. If a leader has not defined each member's role within the vision, they are not completely communicating the direction and not using feedback effectively.

Define what success looks like.

In feedback sessions, assist team member's understanding of their performance by clearly indicating what each member's success can look like. Growing toward success is only possible when they have a clear understanding of what success means in their specific role. It doesn't matter to them what success means to others. It has to be clear to each person. Once they understand success in their terms, they can perform at a much higher ability.

Measure engagement and success.

Highly effective leaders continually set the conditions for success and always provide feedback toward these standards of performance. To be capable of doing so, leaders must build measurement and success goals into the daily actions of each member. Beyond building them, these indicators must always be used on the daily feedback of others, the evaluation processes, and the support strategies used to help team members gain success.

Celebrate each and every person's engagement.

Feedback to great leaders is a chance to help others "get better", improve their own performance, and lead the organization to greater performance. However, they use celebration as a method of encouraging the behavior they wish to see from team members. Celebration of teams, the organization, and working groups is very important. However, leaders will gain a tremendous amount of respect, influence, and commitment by spending the time to give each member a chance to hear directly from you on their performance. Celebrate their wins as though they were yours too.

EXAMPLE

As I previously shared, I was asked to open a new high school. Alignment with the fundamental vision of our organization was of primary importance. We sought to align students' support with every aspect of our school. Our vision was to ensure that EVERY student was successful. To do so, support structures, strategies, and processes had to all align with that goal. I made sure that all of the facets of our program lined up with the acronyms of GOAL vs. GOAT. This acronym meant "Getting Obvious About Learning" as opposed to "Getting Obvious About Teaching". I explained that it didn't matter how many times a concept was taught. It did not matter what material a teacher used to achieve the learning goal. It wasn't relevant which strategy it took for a group of kids to learn. All that mattered was that it was learned and achieved.

This concept also applied to other processes within our organization. We sought results, but focused on the processes we learned that were highly effective toward our vision. This alignment was key to us becoming one of the top high schools in the country. Success has resulted in the areas of academics, arts, and athletics. This framework was, I feel, a tremendous reminder to be creative, flexible, and focused on the vision.

Lead by Delegating

"The best leader is the one who has sense enough to pick good men to do what he wants done. And the self-restraint to keep from meddling with them while they do it." Theodore Roosevelt

BOTTOM LINE

Emerging leaders grow from receiving objective, descriptive growth feedback and applying it in context then debriefing with their leader to connect learning to action. There is only one way for this to happen. Highly effective leaders need to teach others, delegate responsibilities to them, and let them work. Next, they give them descriptive feedback for them to use as growth tools. When giving tasks and actions for emerging leaders to do, leaders need to consider the goals they have for each growing leader and the abilities they have and the learnings they have taught them. This is called delegation. It is a complete process to grow emerging leaders. Simply giving a team member a task to complete is not delegation. Delegating is involved for the leader as they monitor several aspects for learning, completion, and effectiveness. Poor leaders will give others a task and never follow up. Emerging leaders need the follow up to grow.

SUCCESS INDICATORS

Teach them well.

Great leaders that grow emerging leaders use teaching as a significant technique to grow them. They are always looking for topics, methods, and techniques to grow them. Teaching is a useful thought as emerging leaders are only taught by content and feedback. The phrase from my podcast, The Lodge of Leaders, *"Experience is not the best teacher, feedback is..."* is applicable here. Give emerging leaders lessons on how to lead, place them in opportunities to use this knowledge and then provide them with adequate descriptive feedback. This technique works in a variety of areas.

Set and align a vision with your team.

This section may seem like a broken record, but this concept is crucial. Setting and aligning vision with your team members is vital for many aspects of growing leaders and effective leadership. Consider a vision for an organization similar to a learning target for a student. They must know where they are going to be able to attain the achievement of success.

Let team members do their work.

Once emerging leaders have been giving solid instruction in how to lead, and then there has been a context (issue, problem, task) to accomplish, let them do their work. Instruction on the methods of leading as well as the techniques of management and education-specific content is vital. Great leaders will allow emerging leaders to wrestle with issues and even come close to disaster by letting them work. However, they won't let failure become fatal.

Give them descriptive feedback everyday.

Highly effective leaders will monitor and support these emerging leaders as they progress. Of course, we never want to allow anyone to completely fail, but there is growth to be attained by mistakes and then providing solid feedback and self reflection. Debrief will always follow and result from emerging leaders taking action. Build the habit of self reflection and debrief among members you wish to grow. This step is critical in their development.

Feed the culture of feedback among members of your team.

Great leaders will develop feedback as a language all to its own in an organization. They will use every opportunity to grow leaders in their skill sets by giving continual formative assessment along the way to succeeding. This continual use of feedback will develop a culture of giving one another feedback. Once the team members are comfortable giving one another feedback, feedback will be easily taken by members. The resulting culture will be highly collaborative, collegial, and improvement-focused.

EXAMPLE

My role as leader of a large learning organization is to set the conditions for success and give descriptive feedback. The challenge is to not only finish the "work" each day, but to set the foundation of expectations through the setting of conditions and providing feedback. The leaders I am intending to grow are going to be doing various tasks and plans that we have determined prior. I will delegate to them once they have learned the necessary prerequisite skills and the methods necessary to be successful.

I remember a young lady I was eager to grow into a leader. She was a wonderful teacher and very eager, herself, to become a school leader. I briefed her on the aspects of several opportunities for her to grow and tasks she could do to help her growth. One taks she was given was to plan, determine, and conduct the PSAT in our school. The PSAT (Practice Scholastic Aptitude Test) is a rather significant opportunity for kids in our school. All of the sophomores, many of the freshmen and juniors also participate in this test. Annually, we will give nearly 1500 tests. These tests help students do a couple of functions. One, they get practice on a standardized test with accompanying feedback to improve their performance. Two, when they score well they are given opportunities for scholarships and others recognition based upon their performance. The culture of success on this test has been growing each year.

After significant planning, she conducted the administration of the test. To say it didn't go well was an understatement. She put in a lot of work to get ready. However, something was amiss. There was confusion among the kids and the adults administering the test. Albeit confusing, the test was conducted and the students completed their portion of the assessment. After the tests were mailed back, I sought to discuss the scenario with her. To my pleasure, she had already done some serious meta-feedback to assess her strengths and weaknesses in the process. We sat down to debrief. I asked her "How do you think the testing scenario went?" She answered with a resounding "Not well". We then discussed for nearly 30 minutes all of the areas she felt she could improve the testing and her planning processes. She then asked me "Am I going to be fired?". I actually had to laugh. I comforted her by telling her that we all make mistakes, but learning from them is what sets great leaders apart. Mediocre leaders will not assess their losses. Great leaders do just that. They seek to improve after their most troubling performances. This learning could have never occurred if this substantial task had not been delegated to her. Today, she is an outstanding school leader and I am very proud of her.

Lead by Being a Bad-Ass

"If your path demands you walk through hell... Walk as if you own the place."

Gary Davison

BOTTOM LINE

As a leader of an organization, you are the caretaker of others. You are responsible for the students, staff, and community members' well being, learning, and life skills. Ultimately, you determine their trajectory for their futures. This is a tremendous responsibility, but as principal, you gladly accept the challenge. Great leaders know that this is not a burden to be taken lightly. You accept this responsibility with the swagger and confidence of a "protector". I use the term "Badass" to determine what state of mind a leader needs to have when caring for others. In your mind, nothing will hurt or deter your team members from learning and succeeding. When you enter the room or building, it should bring peace and calm to those who are in your charge. They will rely on you and you, as a great leader, need to be up for this challenge and accept it wholeheartedly.

SUCCESS INDICATORS

Take all the slings and arrows for your staff when necessary!

Highly effective leaders who build a culture of collaboration, rely heavily on being a protector for their team members. Ownership is a key indicator for a stellar leader. They will own the mistakes, errors, and poor service when it occurs. However, they will ensure that team members learn how and what to correct to never make these mistakes again. It is based upon learning, but the leader has taken the hit from others when something goes awry. Conversely, highly effective leaders give

184

away the accolades that come their way for success. It's the complaints, criticism, and hateful rhetoric that leaders will accept on behalf of their team members. Ultimately, team members appreciate this as protection from the community toward them.

When someone does something wrong, give them feedback in private!

Giving feedback and constructive criticism is necessary to help others grow. As a leader, this is a vital part of your daily langage. You are always giving alternate methods of accomplishing a task, key factors to consider when planning, and various ways of thinking about planning methods to be the best leader they can grow to be. However, this correction should always be done in private. When a team member needs correction do so in the privacy of their classroom, office, or away from listening ears. This should be a conducive location that they will be at ease and appropriate for learning. Additionally, using language that allows for them to grow and not feel condemned is key. Remember, growth is the goal…not embarrassment.

Shield students from danger at all costs!

As the leader of a learning organization, students are an important group to protect from harm. Always consider yourself as the key protector of the kids. You are in the hallway serving as the "bouncer" for them. Step into fights to keep kids safe, do not allow adults to mistreat them in any way, and be the last line of defense for them. Think of yourself as the one who would take that bullet for each and every student in your school. You are the badass that is there to keep someone's child safe. That mental framework brings calmness and security to parents and will earn you a lot of goodwill. When kids know that you are there to protect them, a level of trust builds and they will be more collaborative and open to learning. Their safety is key.

Endure the scars of protection for others willingly, proudly, and quietly!

Great leaders do not advertise their scars or challenges. They will endure great hardships with a smile on their face and a glint in their eye. The pride they feel enduring FOR their team members is what builds resilience and trustworthiness. These characteristics are very difficult to cultivate, so this is a wonderful way for leaders to build their tribe.

EXAMPLE

I remember being at a basketball game in a rival school. The game was heated with a close rival and there were tense moments. As the score went back and forth, the student sections in the crowd were cheering loudly for their respective teams. I will say that both sets of students were doing a great job being spirited and supporting the players on their teams. It was a cool environment to play in. As the fourth quarter began, an administrator from the opposing team wanted to move our students. I was quite confused as both sets of kids were doing a great job. There was no cursing, calling out of layers, or unsportsmanlike behavior at all. They felt that they were cheering too loudly. Of course, when you are at an opposing school's gym you are subject to the rules that they have in place. However, I was not going to let them affect our kids this way as they were doing a terrific job supporting our team. I let the administrator from the other school know that we were not going anywhere and they could not move us. I was not ugly about it, rather I was matter of fact in my demeanor, but let them know that I would closely supervise our kids.

As their leader, it was my responsibility to stand up and defend our kids for their terrific attitudes and behavior. This request was not right and I would not allow it to stand. Our students were very thankful and showed their support by cheering for me. I did not act upon my defense for their accolades, rather it was to defend my kids.

Summation

To influence others is a privilege and should be taken seriously. The development of great leaders is not rocket science. It is nuanced, complex, and oftentimes, wrought with potholes, difficulties, and tragedies. To become an elite leader who garners the dedication of others, is challenging and yet, easy to do. The skills presented here are just a start toward the development of a leadership skill set that can bring you immense joy. The accumulation of these skills entail the beginning of your journey. Use them as a guide to help you begin to develop skills, hone your current skills, or develop leadership skills in others. Either way, the journey into leadership is a tremendous honor and one that should be considered highly.

Made in United States
Orlando, FL
22 April 2023

32334029R00108